JUXTAPOSITIONS

Harry Rogers

Copyright © 2025 Harry Rogers

All rights reserved.

ISBN: 9798305354447

DEDICATION

To Jenny who continues to put up with me.

CONTENTS

Acknowledgments   i

1   Poems   1

ACKNOWLEDGMENTS

Special thanks to all my followers on my blog at www.harryseeingred.com
Also to the members of Scene Red who keep me in the vein of creativity.
Also to my good comrades in Undod Cwith Cymru and also my fellow writers in The Red Poets, all of whom I admire greatly.
A special mention for all my friends and family who have given me great encouragement in my poetic and songwriting endeavors, I love you all.

1 POEMS

1 - MEDIAGENIC FANTASY

He still believes in Mediagenics,
Like Citizen Kane he thunders onwards,
Spews inexactitudes day in, day out,
Engulfed within his own dark fantasy.
Even as ropes slowly tighten round his neck
Ego dictates he'll get away with it.
When one persistently protests too much,
Sooner or later, ivory towers,
Like remarkable rockets, crash to dust,
Wilderness awaits for giant liars.
Soon gales of mass recognition will blow,
Pennies will drop as old actions will show,
This wolf he cries out about really knows
Sick truths about Trump, and all his oppos.

2nd January 2024.

JUXTAPOSITIONS

2 – PERMANENT S.N.A.F.U.

Starmer stands stiffly in his stuffy suit,
Looks like an old school middle manager.
Prime Minister relaxed in his jumper
Looks like a man who's at ease with himself.
They continue, situation normal,
Election mode donned early by them both.
But nothing is normal, not anymore,
It's all fucked up by Palestine chaos.
How can anyone vote for either one?
Both support Netanyahu's genocide.
Both support more weapons to Israel.
Both support Zionist apartheid.
Neither support Israeli ceasefire.
Can anyone morally vote for them?

5th January 2024.

JUXTAPOSITIONS

3- HUNT DOWN TRUTH SAYERS

Poets, journalists, writers on left wing,
Shoot on sight if they see what's going on.
Oligarchs' mantra? Hide up everything.
Hunt down truth sayers, songs of right and wrong.
Whatever platform where they stand and sing,
Blow them away, before they start their song.

Chop off snowdrop heads hour by hour by hour,
Stop new birth of Spring, keep it underground,
Never let sweetness rise up above sour,
Don't let larks ascend to broadcast free sound,
Obliterate Daffodils in flower,
Bulldoze green shoots of Honesty all round.

Only their propaganda can prevail,
They are God's chosen people after all,
Scripture guides their hand, they can never fail.
They'll ensure those who disagree will fall,
Only their boats will be allowed to sail,
They are special, that's their clarion call.

One thing oligarchs fail to realise
Poets will always highlight rotten lies.

10th January 2024.

4 - THAT OLD FAMILIAR ROAD

Down that old familiar road,
I remember Wellesley Road,
Ain't been there for forty years,
Passed that place where I was born,
In room above saloon bar,
In grandparents public house,
Where my mother kept me warm.
Almost eighty years ago.
Everything is changed today,
Bridge Hotel been swept away,
Spurgeons Bridge, old baptist church,
No trolley bus left to lurch
As it teetered around bends,
Old memories never end.
I can't have too long to go,
Not much time to reminisce,
Life suddenly seems so short,
Not much time left to report.
But I'll do my best somehow,
I'll make time to write it down.

12th January 2024.

5 - SAVE OUR CHILDREN

Is this the way to keep our children safe?
Give support to those who kill young children?
Now full scale annihilation underway.
Truth dribbles out from various sources,
Reports show hidden Zionist intent
To clear Palestinians from Gaza,
To move them south into Sinai desert.
Brazen now they speak out loud of war crimes,
Meanwhile in Den Haag deny genocide,
Take United Nations on a right ride,
One hundred days since bombardment started,
Border locked, imports blocked, freedom blasted.
Shapps ramps up Tory jingo rhetoric,
Electioneering makes me feel quite sick.

15th January 2024.

JUXTAPOSITIONS

6 - PLATE SPINNERS IN CARDIFF BAY

Eluned toes Mark's line again,
There is no money for doctors.
Austerity rules supreme,
Westminster must be obeyed.
Tories pare back subventions,
Welsh Labour cut, slash and burn,
Then bayonet NHS.
In Aberporth drones still fly,
QinetiQ plays with A I.
Transport fails to meet real needs,
Ministers obsessed with speeds,
Can't go out, try as one might,
Buses do not run at night,
No cinema nor theatre,
Music gigs nor poetry.,
Denied to rural carless,
Young and old lumped together
In fantastic harmony.
Time to change Senedd weather,
Leave England altogether,
Listen to People's voices,
Heed democratic choices.
Infrastructure lies undone,
West of Cardiff it's no fun,
For sick and poor race is run,
No matter how plates are spun.

16th January 2024.

JUXTAPOSITIONS

7 - NEWS Vs REALITY

Old king Charlie's prostate gland is swollen,
Twenty five thousand civilians dead.
Trump still claims last election was stolen,
Twenty five thousand civilians dead.
Starmer admits ruthlessness with Corbyn,
Twenty five thousand civilians dead.
Looks like a blanket of snow in winter,
Twenty five thousand civilians dead.
Houtis fire missiles at ships in Red Sea,
Twenty five thousand civilians dead.
Newport to play Manchester United,
Twenty five thousand civilians dead.
Sunak survives pointless Rwanda spat,
Twenty five thousand civilians dead.

18th January 2024

8 - DONKEYS IN PORT TALBOT.

Don't Blame Tata alone in Port Talbot,
For an end to local economy.
Ask why those steelworks aren't nationalised?
Ask who it was brokered a deal with them?
Who privatised British Steel in first place?
Yet another bright Thatcherite idea
That's gone tits up and left workers in lurch.
Now three thousand totally blindsided.
Where's the pre redundancy retraining?
Economic development? What's that?
New Labour implements austerity
As Westminster salami slices all,
As usual gives working class fuck all.
Kinnocks pre election crocodile tears
Go as far as a broken down donkey
With three legs and a Starmerite blindfold.

19th January 2024.

JUXTAPOSITIONS

9 - DOPPELGANGERS IN A STORM

Rain combined with gales is miserable.
Time for a dram or two of malt whisky.
I sit with Naomi Klein's latest book,
Doppelgangers, wide open in my lap.
Gaslit Americans reel from fake news
Spun by hippy marketeers and nazis.
This unholy alliance spreads worldwide
Across digital social media.
Such blatent internet abuse writ large
Opens White House door for demagogue Trump.
Four hundred million American guns
Circulate freely within public hands.
Schools are shot up, children die every week.
Meanwhile send warships to help Israel?

21st January 2024.

10 - LEST WE FORGET

Politicians don't remember at all
Anything that happened, rather forget.
Forget those IDF soldiers who shoot
Children for fun like mice enticed in traps,
Forget wanton cultural destruction
Of library buildings in Palestine,
Forget Universities turned to dust,
Forget writers, musicians and poets
Killed for creatively being just,
Forget slaughter of those beneath white flags,
Forget monstrous bulldozers clearing streets
Of innocent bodies into mass graves.
Forget seventy five years since Nakba,
Forget about those stateless
refugees
Who wait without hope trapped in Al Yarmouk,
Forget our pathetic politicians
Who use selective memory bank books,
Forget all about our own complicity
How we create this dreadful history.
Forget everything about Palestine,
We must get ready for election time.
Sunak v Starmer, plus Biden v Trump,
Collective amnesia out on stump.
There's only one thing left worthy of note,
Forget none of this when we choose to vote.

28th January 2024.

JUXTAPOSITIONS

11 - WHITE FLAG WISDOM

Smarmer says it is unwise for MPs
To watch social media news footage
That shows Israeli defence gun down
A Palestinian with a white flag.
Clearly this is a breach of his precious
International laws, It's a war crime.
No pretence anymore, shown in real time.
Each day death toll ticks up, buildings fall down,
Israel sprays American ordnance
Willy nilly throughout Gaza landscape,
The International Court of Justice
Say South African case is plausible,
Starmers political powder monkeys,
Those former NUS power junkies,
Churn out more soppy campaign one liners,
Designed to appeal to social climbers.
Yet an eerie silence rings in our ears,
No call for ceasefire to end any fears.
What we see is what we get for four years,
An unwise ghoul who bathes in children's tears.

28th January 2024

12 - POP C POP CORN

Get out yer pop corn, here come new Pop Cons,
Popular Conservatives ha, ha ha.
Sound just like National Conservatives.
Nat Cs and their Pop Cs, relaunch too far.
Deluded prophets of Brexit and worse,
Tell us their rehashed crap bedtime stories,
They've stolen our cash, they can't reimburse,
After all at end of day they're Tories,
All they can do is pass mythical blame
Onto woke lefties and sad refugees,
Year after year they're always same old same,
Whilst they force us workers onto our knees.
No more silly Jacob, stupid Liz Truss,
This time round they underestimate us.

7th February 2024.

13 - POINT FINGERS WITH CARE

Point your finger carefully,
Make sure you get it right,
Because if you get it wrong
Then you might start a fight.
Conspiracy is easy,
Fake hares will ever run,
Consequences matter most,
But they're not always fun.
Once triggered, victims fall down,
Theories rain far and wide,
Truth gets lost in mists of time,
Reality trapped inside.
Even worst attrocities
Vanish out of our minds.
Some say they never happened,
Even though you were there,
They'll claim you made it all up,
You'll pull out all your hair.
So when you point a finger
Be careful how you do,
You must always remember
That three point back at you.

7th February 2024.

14 - BBC PECKSNIFFERY

Tell us again about warmed up oceans,
Let us hear about poxy fiscal rules,
Why our chemists have run out of potions,
We need to hear why we're in bed with ghouls.
Where BBC journos reek of Pecksniff,
We're trapped as when someone farts in a lift,
We get sprayed with new oil of techno myth,
No-one loves runners when they finish fifth.
God Save The King plays at end of each night,
I wash my dishes, hands deep in my sink,
Still there's no call for Israeli ceasefire,
Labour frontbench becomes bluest of pink.
Collective amnesia, their silence shouts,
Come election time let's chuck them all out.

13th February 2024.

JUXTAPOSITIONS

15 - CRINKLE CRANKLE POWER WALLS

Pull down those crinkle crankle walls that wind
Inside new new labour supporter minds.
They claim greatest election victory
Since end of world war two for Starmer.
Where sixty two percent plus did not vote?

How hollow empty rhetoric does sound.
McFadden's democracy masquerade
Welcomes turncoat Tories onto parade,
Throwback policies sound so retrograde,
Dig deeper austere holes with Blairite spade.
Where parvenu Streeting shows he believes
Fantasy strategies of Rachel Reeves.

Breakout Kier Starmer's purple custard creams,
As fake fiscal rules trash socialist dreams,
Block out sounds of broken family screams,
From Rafah to Bristol ignore blood streams.
Watch with horror establishment choir
Refuse to support a Gazan ceasefire,
Just when we thought that things couldn't get worse
Neo Liberals tighten strings of purse,
Netanyahu spouts chapters and verses,
IDF shoot dead doctors and nurses.

It's hard to concentrate hour by hour
On crap MPs addicted to power.

16th February 2024.

16 - WHAT WILL THEY SING IN MALMÖ?

Only lonely ghosts remain
Where once their prison stood.
Tens of thousands side by side
Alone as more bombs rain.

Wrecked houses litter safe zones.
In Sinai, near Rafah,
Egypt builds giant camp site
With massive concrete walls.

How many survive next steps
Is an unknown unknown.
What once were family groups
Are become mere remnants.

Even mockingbirds have flown
Nests in this no-fly zone.
Eurovision Song Contest
Happens again come May,

Israelis will sing their song
As if all is normal,
No place there for Palestine,
No dabkas in Malmö,
Just usual grotesque flim flam
Plastic jamboree bag
Filled with jingoistic hype.

This no music festival
Where culture flourishes,
Rather flag waver parade
For rich patriarchies
To wave nationalistic
Willies to hearts content.

Yellow blue Ukrainians
Will compete in this farce,
Along with United Kingdom
Who'll fall flat on its arse.

JUXTAPOSITIONS

What's awful about all this?
There's little we can do,
Cept turn off our TV sets,
Don't whistle Waterloo.

That place we knew as Gaza
By then will not exist,
New settlers will occupy,
They'll all be Zionist.

What will they sing in Malmö?
We'll have to wait and see,
Don't think I'll be listening
It's all too sick for me.

18th February 2024.

17 - WHOSE NEWS?

BBC news tells us thirty thousand
Demonstrate at Israeli embassy,
They call for ceasefire now in Palestine.
Editors leave much to be desired.
It's not just that a quarter million
Marched against genocide and apartheid,
Nor that there were many diverse speakers,
Distortions of reality are par.
Last thing we can expect from state broadcasts
Is any semblance of truth or justice.
All day long preach impartiality,
At same time facts, deliberately skewed,
Miners Strike, Iraq War, spun against each cause,
Journalism stinks of hypocrisy.
Numbers spun auto perfunctorily,
Words, comments, actions shown out of context,
Order of events changed digitally,
Gaslighter wolves dressed up as editors.
Analysis of ideas twists in wind
Whenever our status quo is questioned.
Academic freedom to speak one's mind
Low on list of media super kind.
Be certain, reporters search hard for dirt,
Shoot down messengers before they get heard,
Besmirched, ruined, driven daily away,
No-platformed, scratched out, umpteen shades of grey.
Algorithms flex across internet,
Media control? We've seen nothing yet.
War is love, Lies are peace, Only one god,
Truth is whatever suits today's purpose,
So long as it sticks fast to agenda.
No wonder so many are out of their mind,
Repressive tolerance, dissent flatlined.

19th February 2024.

18 - MOONLIT OR GASLIT?

Clouds of bomb dust swallow full Gazan moon,
Here in West Wales images grow darker,
Bring into focus inhumanity,
Normalcy of torture, blame, maim, shame, game.
End of Ramadan road hoves into view,
Shapeshifter Starmer says not what to do.
Whither young orphans? Where next do they go?
Who's left to love them? Where next will they sleep?
Hospitals shattered, bullets in kids heads,
Doctors can't save those that snipers shoot dead.
Who sold them bullets? Who sold them their guns?
Bunker buster bombs? Let's tot up our sums.
Remnants of families trawl through embers,
Arms company unions count members.
"Follow The Money" what we're always told,
Exploit misery, no love over gold.
Watch on as graffiti fades from brick walls,
War mongers prosper when grim reaper calls.
Back in Palestine a one legged child
Eyes wide with shocked fear, unable to smile,
Stares out from ruins of what once were homes,
Uncomprehends what is meant by safe zones,
As Israeli troops drop leaflets from drones,
Such children face futures bereft of hope.
Adults have failed, we are all complicit,
Some target peace but most humans miss it,
Dollars, euros, pounds and shekels for ghouls,
Capitalism takes us all for fools,
Arms companies prop up economies,
This is what growth means to you and to me.
I'll vote no more for political shits
Who make excuses whilst kids blow to bits.
Some condemn me for being emotive,
Tell me, where next will we sell explosives?
Will there come a time when nobody dies,
When we'll dance neath moonlit Palestine skies?

20th February 2024.

19 - DIGNITY IN INNOCENCE

Heads without bodies, always doomed to fail,
Claim to be moral? They should be in jail.
Arrogant tight rope walkers pirouette
Before they trip and plunge into abyss
Where they crash and burn in full public view.
They treat parliament like N.U.S.,
Most MPs behave as apparatchiks
Swanning around Annual conference,
Play their grubby, stitch up, brownie point games.
Children are obliterated daily,
They have no power, no guilt, no weapons,
They do have dignity in innocence,
Which is a lot more than can be said of
Keir Starmer's Circus of bamboozlement.

22nd February, 2024.

JUXTAPOSITIONS

20 - STARCH UP STUFFED SHIRTS

Same time as Keir Starmer pulled speaker stroke
IDF bombed Rafah, one more sick joke.

On nineteen seventies graffiti wall,
Written clear in black letters four feet tall,
ISRAEL BOMBS PALESTINIAN TENTS,
I read it daily as to work I went.

This slogan remains etched deep on my mind,
Fifty years later and what do we find?
One million people displaced in tents,
With each revelation I'm more incensed,
Mostly their homes have been bulldozed away,
Gaza now Pandemonium today.

Orwell so prescient, he got it right,
Newspeak now spouted each day and each night.
As we get closer to next Ramadan,
Remember Keir Starmer ain't Superman.
He lives in reality that's not real
Works towards maintenance of status quo.

Now in an act straight out of Bizarro,
Peace activists painted as terrorists,
War entrepreneurs profit from terror,
Protest blown up as if revolution,
We're all being collectively punished
For standing up against occupation,
For recognising there's no place like home,
For showing support for children from bombs.

In parliament no democracy,
It's transformed into pure ochlocracy.
Party mobsters run their local fiefdoms,
Obsessed with control of spoken freedoms,
Donations from businesses prop them up.
They find it easy to sell us a pup.

For them modern quislings are true heroes,
Whilst all that they do adds up to zero,
Everything now central control slanted,

JUXTAPOSITIONS

Membership views are taken for granted.
Kier rummages through Johnson's old wardrobe,
He hides Forde report of racism probe.

Rumours abound of new party in March,
Labour hares iron stuffed shirts with more starch.
In Rafah they wait to find out their fate,
Will tanks roll in or Egypt open gates?

Whatever happens it's all a disgrace,
Don't know how Starmer can still show his face.

25th February 2024.

JUXTAPOSITIONS

21 - LAST ZEBRA AT THE ZOO

When we saw the last zebra at the zoo
That was the day I fell in love with you
The other animals were dead and gone
One lonely keeper whistled his sad song

Lost memories fill up empty cages
Where sea lions clapped on silver stages
Elephants carried young kids for a ride
Whilst chimps contemplated their suicide

Last zebra at the zoo
I fell in love with you
Last zebra at the zoo
I fell in love with you

The day to close the zoo has nearly come
All the fences are coming down today
Wilderness belongs to the wild and free
My heart beats louder than a big bass drum

All the hunters have been told go away
Soon I hope that you will be kissing me
When we saw the last zebra at the zoo
That was the day I fell in love with you

Last zebra at the zoo
I fell in love with you
Last zebra at the zoo
I fell in love with you

Harry Rogers, Stresa, Italy.

JUXTAPOSITIONS

22 - FALLING OUT OF LOVE WITH LOVE

Saw the news today, dunno what to say
Dropping barrel bombs where the children play
Sell arms to tyrants just because they pay
We're falling out of love with love today
Yemenis, Syrians, Iraqis, Kurds
All are now victims of misguided words
Those religious partisans tend their herds
Where people once were freer than the birds

I wish they would stop
Falling out of love with love
I wish we could stop
Falling out of love with love

Stop
Falling
Falling out of love with love

My daughter said why can't we get along?
Why can't we all sing the same happy song?
All this senseless killing is so plain wrong
People just want somewhere they can belong
Outsiders look on whilst the wild wind blows
Wen it will end? Well now, nobody knows.
Right across the world we keep on our toes
As all this stupid mayhem grows and grows

I wish they would stop
Falling out of love with love
I wish we could stop
Falling out of love with love

Stop
Falling
Falling out of love with love

Harry Rogers: In Harriboy's Hut, Aberbanc - 22nd September 2016

23 - WHEN PEOPLE VOTE RESIST

I wonder if we can
Remember Vietnam
When protest won the day,
War mongers ran away.
We all sang West Coast songs,
People knew it was wrong.
It's happening again,
We cannot bear such pain .
Israel flies blue flags,
Children rifle trash bags,
MPs cry terrorist
When people vote resist.
We've seen it all before,
When we stand against war.
All we have left is hope,
No Ceasefire? Then no vote.

2nd March 2024.

24 - FEASIBLE PRECAUTIONS

Israeli spokesperson stands
Bold, as ever, at a lectern,
Straight faced he proceeds to tell us
That his government have taken
All feasible precautions to
Avoid deaths of civilians.
Simultaneously his troops
Open fire on hungry people.
What are feasible precautions?
"Feasible precautions" are those
Precautions which are practicable,
Or practically possible
Taking into account all Circumstances ruling at the time,
Including humanitarian and
Military considerations.
Are we to believe naked lies?
Bunker buster bomb raids are not
Compatible with this statement,
Neither is cutting off water,
Destroying public services,
Bulldozing houses, schools, and shops.
Five months of state terror tactics,
Thirty thousand plus dead people,
Seventy thousand more wounded,
Many more missing presumably dead,
This is nowhere near to taking
Feasible precautions, is it?
How can you take such actions
When you know there is nowhere to run?
Feasible is the wrong word where
These war mongers are concerned.
A truer descriptor would be
Risible, after what we've all seen.
That's it, risible precautions,
And I don't even believe them.

4th March 2024.

25 - GET YOUR COATS

One hundred and fifty days of terror,
Inflicted on collateral targets,
This is total torture ramped up to max.
It's gone beyond popular forgiveness.
Out of control occupational force
Inflicts mental horror without a thought.
Fear, writ large across faces of children,
Whose trust in adult normalcy destroyed,
Driven forward by entitled belief
That they are chosen above all others.

Victims now victimisation experts
Dedicated to increased victimhood
Of innocents trapped inside bomb alley.
Meanwhile, down in depths of old London town,
You arrive at parliament by car,
Sit on green benches, spout meaningless words
About importance of democracy.
You front benchers take your joint decisions
To carry on sales of weapons abroad,
To Tel Aviv and other war mongers,
Tell the whole world how Israel must win.

When we baulk at your outrageous attempts
To convince us of our complicity,
Through your arrogant abuse of language,
By saying out loud no ceasefire no vote,
You appear in media studios
And accuse us of being terrorists.

As each one hundred and fifty days passed
We understood truthful reality,
Pictures of destruction became clearer,
We who campaign for peace and justice
Are not, and never have been, terrorists,
Terrorism is exercised en masse
By artificial democrats who take
Their voters for granted and ignore peace.

Will rivers carry freedom to the sea?
Will Palestine exist for you or me?

JUXTAPOSITIONS

This is a matter which comes to a crux,
Now it is time to end this state of flux.
Minute by minute, hour by hour,
We work each day to remove your power.
That's why we all say No Ceasefire No Votes,
Your time has run out, now please get your coats.

5th March 2024.

26 - PORT GASLIGHT

Joe poses, cornet in hand,
Proposes Gazan sea port,
Thinks none of us understand,
Gaslit pre-election sport.
As we head towards Ramadan,
Threats grow stronger day by day,
Every child, woman and man,
Could easily be blown away.
Two months to set up pontoon,
And cranky new supply chain,
Might as well send food to moon,
Increase genocidal pain.

Some things hard to understand,
Stàrk real life does not compute,
Want to feed people on land?
What's wrong with weaponry route?
Yankee ordnance trades OK,
Bullets, bombs arrive each day,
Mostly made in USA,
It's hard to know what to say.
Israel set up blockade,
Biden decides to pierce it,
Blood flows on inside stockade,
No dead Gazan child hears it.
Senate cheers Joe's every word,
Netanyahu spews more shite,
Days polishing up this turd,
Roll out shiny Port Gaslight.

9th March 2024

27 - REMNANTS REMAIN

Those dead journalists laid out in Gaza
No longer write about truth they have seen.
Yet we who stand up for freedom of speech,
Who cannot sit meekly silenced at home,
Will very soon be deemed to be extreme
By abusers of faux democracy.
Orwellian imagination spewed
From pens filled with blood streaked, bigotted, bile
In full blown fountainhead of newspeak laws
Gove shoots from crooked conservative lip.
Those who stand against obliteration,
Who dare to make their joined up voices heard,
Face enforced silence in fear of prison
By those who are not about to listen.
One hundred and eighty dead in Gaza,
Wiped out for speaking real truth to power,
Strong journalists who refused to cower.
There remains a failure to understand
Whilst you can destroy child, woman or man,
No matter how hard legal eagles try
They cannot legislate away ideas
Of truth, of justice,, of freedom, of peace.
We'll gather on streets in greatest number,
Like Shelley's lions, arose from slumber.

March 2024.

28 - LUNACY IN EXTREMIS

Stand up for and against democracy
In simultaneous volte face display
Of utter lunacy in extremis.
These old former FCS activists
In their Hang Nelson Mandela tee shirts
Wreak giant Thatcherite hornswoggle schemes
And we're supposed to swallow all of them.
Inflation has fallen, NHS fixed,
We need new North Sea Oil fields to survive,
Sunak and Hunt smirk over front bench stunts,
Point fingers at Labour dopplegangers,
All of them riding two horses at once,
Replete after downing subsidised lunch.
Lobbyists, journos, old back bench liggers,
Can barely contain hard hearted sniggers,
Sped up spads deliver new fake figures,
Westminster sways with waltzers and jiggers.
We are expected to give them our votes,
Not this time! We've seen how they pocket notes,
Give contracts to mates, to old school tie scrotes,
Beats me how this rotten ship of state floats.

Harry Rogers in the Red Bedroom 20th March 2024.

29 - CLAP OUT THE OLD

They clap out the old, then clap in the new,
Nothing will change for me nor for you.
Democracy fails, it's so sinister,
People have no say in first minister.
Cardiff becomes clone of Westminster,
In hock to bankrupted House of Windsor.
Future like past is mapped out, still austere,
Salami slice services whilst they cheer.
Decimate libraries, shut toilets down,
Make Sunak's cuts in each village and town.
Test UAV weapons for Israel,
Help turn Palestine into living hell.
Out on our streets cost of living gets worse,
AMs sail on through clapped out universe.
Steel workers quake as redundancy calls,
Old Labour support collapses, then falls.
These days are bad and poised to get darker.
Why wait, arms outstretched, we must get smarter.

20th March 2024

JUXTAPOSITIONS

30 - YES IN MY BACK YARD

Yes In My Back Yard
Sing me some old songs
That bind me like spells
Help me right some wrongs
Blow my mind away
I will take a chance
Bring changes we need
Dance that yimby dance.

Yimby yimby dance
Yimby yimby dance
Dance dance yimby dance
Yimby yimby dance

We'll dance very hard
Dance to understand
What is going on
Play loud yimby band.
Help us help you now
We all feel your pain
Come now dance with us
You can dance again.

Yimby yimby dance
Yimby yimby dance
Dance dance yimby dance
Yimby yimby dance

Yes in my back yard
Dance in my back yard
Smile in my back yard
Live in my back yard
Love in my back yard
Here in my back yard

Yimby yimby dance
Yimby yimby dance
Dance dance yimby dance
Yimby yimby dance

23rd March 2024

31 - SEA VIEW IN GAZA

Every day's a hot day on Gazan coast,
Settlers get ready to stake out their claims,
Israel Defence Force bulldozers roll,
Palestinians have nowhere to turn.
It's hard to work out what hurts most of all,
Is it naked glee from those who move in?
Or famine wrecked children dead by sea shore?
Ghoulish desire for prime real estate,
Built atop rubble from American bombs.
Brutal acquisitiveness shames us all,
Seen it before over past centuries,
Smallpox laced blankets given to Shawnees,
Poisoned indigenous Australians,
Bengali starvation by Churchill's command,
For aeons humans butcher each other,
We claim to be totally civilised,
Of course we ain't, barbarism still rules.
This our conundrum, where lies decency?

25th March 2024

JUXTAPOSITIONS

32 - WHAT LIES BENEATH CLOUDS?

Fly high above brilliant sun lit whiteness,
What lies beneath obscured from naked view?
Taken for granted England is below,
A thought niggles, perhaps it's not there.
Maybe a i auto-pilot cracked up,
And we have changed course without our knowledge,
Head out towards unknown ocean splashdown.
How easily we hand our existence
Over to new modern technology.
We believe most technocratic bullshit,
We are all post office managers now,
Taken for rides in futuristic schemes,
Designed to convince us that all is well,
Except when it goes tragically wrong.
Speaker voice says we are about to land,
We descend beneath clouds, runway in view,
All is tickety boo, Bristol is near.
Everything goes like clockwork, smoothly we land.
Meanwhile, Baltimore cargo ship crashes,
Technology fails, giant bridge splashes.
I walk through rain into new arrivals,
Pleased to be here, safe this time, this time, safe……

27th March 2024.

33 - How Wretched Is Life Become?

How wretched is life become
For those forced into harms way?
Wracked with fear of sniper fire,
Discharged at any moment,
Indiscriminately spread
At any sign of movement.
Young men shot dead, then bulldozed,
Their identity unchecked.

New orphaned child amputees,
No health care facilities,
Only most abject wreckage.
Not fit for any purpose.
Americans talk of aid,
Of an end to bombardment
Whilst they vote weapon supplies.
Such overt hypocrisy
Takes what's left of breath away.
Deliberate starvation?
Send them more bunker busters.
More collective punishment?
Repair their F thirty fives.
Rampant diseases run wild?
Send in more ammunition?

Cameron spins truth away,
After all we need arms trade,
Don't we? Need fucking arms trade?
As Ramadan heads to end
This ghastly catastrophe
Morphs into the essence of
Genocide before our eyes.
Pandemonium on speed,
Rafah will not survive.
Is this what Sunak meant? Eh?
Or Starmer when they both said
Israel must win? Must win?
What is such a victory?

Sociopathic nightmare,
Committed on a grand scale,

JUXTAPOSITIONS

A brazenly wrought war crime.
Psychologically bent
Politicians wag fingers
For they are always right on,
Aren't they? Right on? Always? Eh?

Painted into this corner
Murderers have no way out,
Until they have no-one to kill.
Such are these theatres of war
That we are all paying for.........

2nd April 2024

34 - NOTHING LEFT

Total annihilation is their goal.
They will wipe out Gaza once and for all.
What other reasons are there for these acts?

Nobody will be able to live there
When an armistice comes into being.

No municipal infrastructure left,
No public health care facilities left,
No educational establishments,
Hardly any residential homes left.
No water or sewage systems are left.

It is absolutely clear in my mind,
This is systematic ethnic cleansing
Of Palestinians out of Gaza.

I can find no other explanation.

4th April 2024

35 - LAVENDER BLUES, DILLY, DILLY

Rotten stench of lavender hangs heavy
Across early evening Gazan sunset.
Not that lavender we all know and love
That grows in fields and gardens everywhere.

This lavender stench comes as a result
Of dead bodies that rot beneath rubble.
These bodies dead because AI software
Identified young men as combatants,
Based upon how they fit algorithmic
Designed profiles. What is this software called?

It's called LAVENDER, hence this ghastly stench.
Everywhere we hear people call this war.
This industrial, technological
Psychological, genocidal shit
Is not a war. It is autonomy
Delivered collective mass murder.

Lavender Blues, Dilly, Dilly
Lavender Blues

Will we ever see a free Palestine?
When will we ever sing this old folk tune?

"Let the birds sing, dilly, dilly
And the lambs play
We shall be safe, dilly, dilly
Out of harm's way."

Lavender Blues, Dilly, Dilly
Lavender Blues.

4th April 2024

36 - ONLINE IMMORTALITY

You know you're old when blog follower friends
Die almost every week while you rant onwards.
Out there, on internet, people live on,
Even though they're already cremated,
They smile out at you from their Facebook page
As if you could walk round their house right now,
Sit down, and carry on that discussion
You've been in debate with them forever.
Trouble is you look older, they don't change.
Years go by and they look younger each time
They pop up in your photo memories.
They toast you with a glass of wine held high,
Brandish their guitar with total intent,
And as for videos? They're even worse.
Not only do they look young, so do you.
But, it is nice, sometimes, to reminisce,
All those good times, and those wild adventures,
Just make sure you can't see any mirrors.
Well not for a few minutes in any case,
By which time you'll have scrolled on to Scrabble.

6th April 2024.

37 - REMEMBER JAVA MONKEY

I remember Java Monkey,
Coffee bar in Decatur town.
So glad I got to read in there,
Not long before it was burnt down.
That place where poets, black and white,
Read their work on true open mic,
Each race and gender given flight,
To read their words how they did like.
I was truly blown clean away,
Atlanta Georgia's mirror shone,
I heard freedom's voice upon that day,
I realised that I'd been wrong.
Just because I was in Deep South
Did not mean people are cut outs,
That Presidential motor mouth
Does not reflect truth when he spouts.
Now, even though building is gone,
Where truth and beauty did belong,
Poets continue to write strong,
Java Monkey's spirit lives on.

7th April 2024.

38 - LIGHT BRIGHT LANTERNS

Light lanterns and search in those dark corners.
Those places where secrets are long hidden.
Now is exactly right time to ferret
Out fiddles, scams, shady deals, bent bastards,
Political corruption, stuff like that.
Hold grifters feet to fires whilst backs are turned.
Turn our spotlights to maximum brightness,
Scrutinise every single candidate
Before they get hands on power levers.
Otherwise we all know what happens next,
We saw it through our covid raddled eyes.
Billions syphoned from public accounts
Into untendered contractor pockets.
Set up microscopes, it's election time…..
Again.

8th April, 2024.

39 - X MARKS SPOT

In lands without laws oligarchs roam free,
To say what they want and do as they please.
Beyond control they cry "freedom of speech",
But hardly ever practice what they preach.

Algorithms limit how data spreads,
It has to conform with what's in their heads.
What's the point of building up lists of friends
If you can only contact up to ten?

They allow liars to spread wide their bile,
Do deals with regimes that steal country miles.
Look at endless adverts they feed ya,
No longer is this true social media.

X marks spot where communication died,
Where deep fakes became rudely monetised.

8th April 2024

40 - ETONIAN PIGEON ON A STOOL

There he sits, Etonian Foreign Sec,
In front of press, he shows us his brass neck.
We will not cancel Israeli arms sales,
He's been assured that our laws will not fail,
Legal advisors say needn't worry.

Ramadan ends soon, Bulldozers scurry,
Front line IDF, batteries recharched,
Will surge into Rafah, egos enlarged.
We will all have blood splashed over our hands,
Collective punishment, I understand,
Comes with collective responsibility.

Where's our democratic nobility?

Yesterday's man, a pigeon on a stool,
Unelected now takes us all for fools.

10th April 2024

41 - BIRTH OF REBELLION 1960

Mr Jenkins struts in dingy study
With his cane held tightly in his right hand.
"Stand on that spot, face that wall, bend over."
I comply meekly, he thrashes six times.

Silently tears roll down my flushed red face.
I have committed that most heinous crime,
I did not hand in my homework on time.
This is not first time, neither is it last,
As I leave my mind is filled with anger,
Hatred for authority, disrespect.

Unchastened, confused, unloved, in great pain,
Six thick welts throb simultaneously,
It hurts to sit down, I stand in playground,
Look through his window, rebellion grows.

17th April 2024

42 - BOAT VOTES

On with Tory motley propaganda
Planes soon will fly off to Rwanda.
Desperate refugees put in harms way,
Demonstrate what we have become today.
All these poor people now tarred with same brush,
Calls for human rights reduced to a hush,
Yellow press moguls push fascist demands,
Happily Sunak enacts their commands.
Get it all done before we go to polls,
Treat all boat people as if they're rag dolls.
Humanity dies with fear of other,
Protesters now will all run for cover.
We sell weaponry that fuels foreign wars,
Refuse to accept how partly we cause
Conditions that lead so many to flee,
Can't we accept responsibility?

23rd April 2024.

43 - ETERNITY'S GATE

Eternity's gate remains propped open,
Blocked by thousands of tons of bomb rubble.
Each day more desperate people fall through
Into early sorrow filled extinction.

We chronicle mass mental destruction
With fewer expressions of felt outrage
From media wonks and mainstream leaders.

Familiarity born contempt aimed
Not at genocidal practitioners,
Instead target civilised protesters
Whilst more attrocities are discovered,
And weaponry contracts do multiply,
Whilst depressed families break down and cry
As they watch their children curl up and die.

27th April 2024

JUXTAPOSITIONS

44 - IMMOLATION

He burns himself outside Donald's trial,
His theory of conspiracy in flames,
Now unknown across planet, such a waste.

Meanwhile Donald sleeps on as case unfolds,
Awakes for daily press conference speech,
Demeans rule of law with every breath,
Believes rules do not apply in his case,
Each utterance fuels bonfires of justice,
Ultimate nihilist practice underpins
Insane MAGA Crowleyesque behavior.

Do what Trump wilt shall be whole of Trumps law,
One day orange heads will burst into flames,
Paper evidence mountain grows higher,
Yet, still, this monster stokes funeral pyre.

25th April 2024.

JUXTAPOSITIONS

45 - TORY REFUGEES WELCOME HERE

Wes calls for Tories to join him and Kier.
Can't you tell, it's election year?
Save NHS, join them today?
Read between lines, look what they say.
Private health care OKAY with them,
Blairite blue skies over again.
Tories and Labour gloss past lies,
Dodgy cement, shite PFIs,
Send patients into marketplace,
Service slow tracked by sick cash chase,
Bevan, distraught, spins in his grave,
Free health for all too late to save.
Rishi and Wes both holiday,
With health jackals from USA.

28th April 2024.

JUXTAPOSITIONS

46 - Haiku To New Phone

New phone came today
It's already total love
It's blown my small mind

2nd May 2024

47 - FLUFF AND FLUMMERY

Eurovision Song Contest comes around,
Where camp fluff and flummery doth abound.
Behind scenes song hacks churn propaganda,
Flags and banners on hotel verandahs,
Nationalism underpins glitz and gloss,
Glown up harlequins spout meaningless dross.
Portrayed as harmless extravaganza,
Ghost politics infect many stanzas.
This is a time for us to wonder why
An apartheid state is allowed to try
And portray itself without any fuss
As if Israel can be one of us.
Whilst Gazan atrocities trundle on
We're expected to applaud Zion's song.

5th May 2024.

48 - CROSSFIELDS MEMORY '78

In summer of nineteen seventy eight,
Another warm Saturday post gig night,
We sit in a Crossfields Estate kitchen.
Count Waldronski, Bo and I drink cold beers.

There is a strong air of optimism,
We discuss politics late towards dawn.
Dave is certain that change is gonna come,
Greenpeace will lead environmental change,
His eloquence on that night stays with me,
I remain convinced that David was right,
We needed green socialism back then,
And we need it even more in these times.

Dave shone like only true activists can,
Put life at risk on Rainbow Warrior,
Always stood for workers rights all his life.
That night we didn't foresee Thatcher's reign,
Nor those Blairite wars or Cameron's pain.

Our belief in change remains, never wrong.
Even now, though Count Waldronski has gone,
In our memory his spirit lives on.
I'll not forget you Dave, I remember.

8th May 2024

JUXTAPOSITIONS

49 - LOCK AWAY LAWNMOWERS

From Rafah to Ramallah and Jenin
Israelis ride giant bulldozers,
Scrape bodies and rubble from stolen land.
Use sick metaphor, don't misunderstand,
When they say it's time to "mow lawn" again,
This means slow genocide, more drawn out pain.

Each Palestinian generation
Denied their right to become a nation.
From New Cross to Oxford students stand tall,
Solidarity slogans large on walls.

Westminster spin doctors have us believe
Sunak and Starmer's right to deceive.

Truth though is plain to see, black is not white,
We'll stand proud, we'll protest, for human rights.

9th May 2024.

50 - AURORA BOREALIS IN ABERBANC (Haiku)

Aberbanc soldier
Surfs against Northern Lights Sky,
Unexpectedly.

11th May 2024.

JUXTAPOSITIONS

51 - IS RAFAH AN END GAME?

They bombed
Hospitals,
Libraries,
And Universities.
Waterworks,
Sewage works,
And children in their beds.
Food markets,
Olive groves,
And all their restaurants.
Bus stations,
Chemist shops,
And healthcare surgeries.
They killed
Journalists,
Aid workers,
Doctors and nurses too.
Grandmothers,
Grandfathers,
And their grandchildren too.
Schoolteachers,
Professors,
And their young students too.
Farm workers,
Shop keepers,
And taxi drivers too.
Musicians,
Stage actors,
And anyone that moved.

In occupied Gaza
There's nowhere left to hide,
Clearly we all can see,
That this is genocide.

Is Rafah an end game?
Have our brains turned to shit?
To say and do nothing
Makes us all complicit.

13th May 2024.

52 - ANIMUS IN DUMA

Driven by vengeance settlers storm Duma,
They leave burned out cars and houses behind.
Children lie immolated in their beds,
Parents roasted to death in this madness.

At same time in Malmo insanity
Ignored as motley continues to prance.
Premier league dominates news programmes,
Tory defectors fill up spare headlines.

Late night parties rave beneath Northern lights.
Starmer's future appears far less rosy,
As his blunder has pissed off so many,
His lack of political acumen
Now is treated with total derision
By discerning voters across all sides.

How soon will general election come?
Will pollsters read public changes in mood?
Power of media faces big test,
Propaganda silos run on empty,
This time it's really up to you and me,
Slick politicians run into trouble,
Those children buried neath Gazan rubble.

14th May, 2024.

53 - ARMAGEDDON PLAYBOOK

Orange Antichrist, impassively waits,
As courtroom saga meanders onwards.
We glean Stormy's odd salacious titbits
That conjure up sad naughty boy antics.
She spanked his ass with rolled up magazine,
I betcha it wasn't Woman's Weekly.

Evangelical hordes catastrophise
Whilst they dole out their rapturous applause,
They chant MAGA MAGA MAGA as they
Dream rivers of blood on Plains of Sharon.

Donald, personified as Jesus Christ,
Wields revelatory sword of revenge,
So that fundamentalists can achieve
Final prophecy through Armageddon.

17th May 2024.

54 - DEMOCRATIC ILLUSION

Everywhere we look oligarchs abound,
Their influence exists beyond control.
Their business interests served without a sound,
They play corporate games of whack-a-mole.

Whenever opposition rears it's head
Paid officials of state soon smash it down,
Aided by media until it's dead,
No longer able to make any sound.

Out on our streets they send in their forces,
To rip up our banners, tear down our tents,
Billy clubs, tear gas, armour clad horses,
If that doesn't work build barbed wire fence.

Every five years set up election zones,
Play daily with words, spread mass confusion,
If wrong side gets in? They send in their drones.
It's part of democratic illusion.

It's a free country, ain't it?
Well, ain't it?

21st May 2024.

JUXTAPOSITIONS

55 - THE BOY WHO WONDERED WHY?

I sat beside swimming pool with a towel across my shoulder,
I undid a packet of glucose sweets that my aunt had given me.
I was wet and got colder after i came second in my heats,
I saved myself for those finals later that afternoon.
I looked out of a window and watched a flock of geese fly by,
I stared at bright blue sky and i started to wonder why?

Wondered why?
Wondered why?
I was the boy who wondered why?

Why it is I'm always at these galas on my own?
Why it is I always find I am home alone?
Why no one is ever there when I do something I like?
Why no one can remember first time I ever rode a bike?
Why when I'm a good swimmer I never gets to go on boats?
Why it is I always get given second hand overcoats?
Why it is my dad never sees me doing things at which I'm good?
Why ever did it take me so long before I knew I understood?

I wondered why?
Wondered why?
Wondered why?

Why should ever I go back to that place that they call home?

Wondered why?
Wondered why?

Why it is that I know now is right time to say goodbye.....
Whilst I sit beneath that window and gently start to cry.

23rd September 2012, Reworked 21st May 2024

56 - DON'T ARM AGED DON

Aged Don stands, in dock, accused of fraud,
His supporters believe him innocent,
All charges obviously trumped up fakes.
State lawyers conspire in Boogaloo brains.

This circus of legal jugglers and clowns
Turns New York's justice system upside down.
Crowds look on with abject fascination,
As each day this con man paints new face on.

November poll rushes ever closer,
Silly hair do hid by red MAGA cap,
Loudly preposterous gaslight techniques
Rouse evangelical proud boys and geeks.

Whatever happens don't arm aged Don,
'Cos if you do you'll get Armageddon.

23rd May 2024.

57 - INDEPENDENCE ELECTION

Behind rain soaked lectern day
Rishi's wishes washed away
Angry Tories bite their tongues
Sun Election this way comes.
Labour rabbits in headlights
Change, their one word slogan. Right?
They revert to Blairite guff
As if we want to hear such stuff.
Change to days of Iraq War,
To PFI disaster,
Blue sky thoughts back on table,
Tory converts enabled.
TINA's shoulders shrugged on streets
BBC runs old repeats,
But there's something new in air,
A warning whiff they don't share,
People peel back Kier's cover,
Shocked at what they discover,
Swivel eyed monster within,
Chameleon changed in skin.
Pledges, promises, all gone,
Smiles as if there's nothing wrong.
We remember all his lies,
His sneaky fake alibis,
How he besmirched true comrades,
Avoided our barricades.
Now he implores for our votes,
After he has sunk our boats.
But now there's another way,
New Labour has run it's day,
Independence is in sight,
Reject Starmer and the right,
As their deckchairs rearrange,
Socialists can bring true change.
We can make Fourth of July
Independent if we try.

24th May 2024

58 - S T O P !

Every number is a person,
Every person counts for something.
Streets of buildings come, buildings fall,
In greater schemes buildings mean fuck all.
Humans buried beneath rubble
Creates real traumatic trouble.
Especially those innocents
Now being bombed inside their tents.
One or millions horrify,
All barbarism makes me cry.
Now we're inside election race,
Main candidates avoid this space,
Keep their campaigns mainly local,
Keep away from multi-focal,
Say nothing of those blown to bits
Inside safe zones by lunatics.
Those Tory-Labour little shits,
Know that they are all complicit.
Keep death factories churning out
Tools of murder. I want to SHOUT
STOP IT, STOP IT, STOP IT, STOP IT,
STOP KILLING KIDS WHO CAN'T ESCAPE!.
STOP FILLING UP OUR WORLD WITH HATE!
I know they won't listen to me,
One old man writing poetry,
But write I must, I'm filled with pain,
I'll never vote for them again.

27th May 2024

59 - BULLY BOYS

All those Bullingdon Club right hons
Are now Tory Party write offs.
Their arrogant Oxford poses
Whilst they looked down powdered noses.
Fancy dressed privileged boneheads
Burned fivers in front of homeless.
High testosterone falluted,
Their braincells badly polluted,
For them these were their good old days,
Smashed up restaurants? Parents paid!
We suffer from their damage done
These bully boys were never fun.
Still onwards motley, ever on,
New clowns like them still sing same songs.
This was favoured fact, not fiction,
Imagine them in conscription.

29th May 2024.

JUXTAPOSITIONS

60 - WAYWARD CATS

I came across a herd of cats,
I watched them as they knitted fog.
Not one of them knew where it's at,
Again they all fell off their log.

They hissed and screeched around, around,
Bared sharpened claws then took a pounce,
Never heard such a dreadful sound,
Send catnip quick, at least an ounce.

Their bold experiment now done,
They prowl around and hunt fresh mice,
Cradle strings broke now every one,
Fake ideology advice.

Once they did rule as jungle kings,
Saw clearly throughout darkest night,
But cats can be such real strange things,
Lose focus, can't tell wrong from right.

In order now to save my soul,
I'll nip downtown and spend some cash,
Buy them a brand new scratching pole,
For these are not coolest of cats.

3rd June 2024

JUXTAPOSITIONS

61 - JIVE NIGHT IN ARLES

Two hares jive on a starry starry night,
On fresh mown hay near Vincent's Cyprus tree.
Once in a while you might see such a sight,
As a cloudless sky light swirls heavenly.

Oh how luscious their guitar music sounds,
Whilst they play all night like Buddy Holly,
They spin each other round and round and round,
These are those times when we all feel jolly.

It's a jive night in Arles

One more jive night in Arles

Pour me some more absinthe please, keep me here,
In this visionary world, half past three,
Forget those modern horrors, escape fear,
Prancing with these animals, truly free.

It's a jive night in Arles

One more jive night in Arles

Merge eighteen eighties with nineteen fifties,
Merge eighteen eighties with nineteen fifties,
Merge eighteen eighties with nineteen fifties,

Where we can sing and dance and shake our ears....

One more jive night, in Arles.

4th June 2024.

62 - HARVEST YOUNG FLOWERS

Compulsory coercion
Conservative corruption
Obligation slavery
Artificial bravery
Loudly knock upon our doors
Must obey new written laws
Take our orders from above
Counteract old peace and love
False leadership conflicted
Flowers of youth conscripted
Don't you dare think for yourself
Burn those books from off your shelf
Harvest young minds to capture
For Armageddon rapture
Make all our lives uniform
Wish that we had not been born
Forget creativity
Reinvent nativity
Rishi's National Service
Thin edge of hard right wing wedge.

6th June 2024

63 - BANGED UP IN A KILL ZONE

When you are banged up inside a kill zone,
As days and months pass by
Obliteration becomes usual,
People lose their will to cry.

Survival slowly deteriorates
Without means to carry on,
Explosions broadcast daily on our screens.
This becomes a normal wrong.

Homes are mostly uninhabitable,
Sanctuary hard to find,
Nobody knows where it's safe to shelter,
Doobis never far behind.

Trapped like so many fish in a barrel,
Precision combat from drones,
There is no escape, no place left to hide,
Banged up inside a kill zone.

8th June 2024.

64 - ONE TIME IN DEVON

I sit in my hotel bar with a beer,
A plate of burritos and herb fried rice.
Three Bovey boys drink cider in their seats,
They're regaled by a Florida swamp thing.
At first, this thirty five year old monster,
Tells of eight packs of illegal baccy
In his carrier bag, bought just today.
Somehow he engineered conversation
Onto young men, money, and lots of guns.
When, at eighteen, he got a high paid job.
"I bought so many guns it was heaven."
I'm quietly annoyed by his bombast.
When he blames Joe Biden for his son's crimes
I interject, "Do you blame your father
For those mistakes you made when you were young?"
"Well……no," he drawls, "but Biden is dreadful."
"Not as dreadful as the alternative."
I counter. He pauses then he spits back,
"Trump will fit in better with oligarchs
Who run our planet." And names five leaders.
"Sit them all in a locked room full of guns,
Make them play a game of Russian roulette.
When they're finished and they are all wiped out
This world would then be a much safer place."
He hurrumphed, then said, "Guess you might be right."
He turned away, I drank last of my beer,
Left him proselytising on pistols,
Whilst I went and bought two poetry books.
Twenty twenty four feels like a weird year,
Things seem to be slightly out of kilter.

13th June 2024

65 - WHAT ARE WE?

Billions of suns, are we all alone?
What kind of beings have humans become?
Fermi's paradox asks where are they?
Those others out there in multi-verses?
I think we need to answer What are we?
Two hundred and sixty nine days non stop,
Mass destructive dehumanisation,
Chaos that leads to such utter despair.

Twelve year old girl looks after her sisters,
Extented family already dead,
Blown to pieces before her very eyes
By an American made bunker bomb.
She has no shelter, nowhere to shower,
No kitchen, no belongings, nothing left,
Only her younger sisters have survived.
They are forever hungry and thirsty,
No longer scared by explosions or drones,
All pervasive smell of death now normal.

She hopes they will die in tonight's air raid,
Then, at last, this nightmare will be over.
Meanwhile we turn telly on from sofa,
Watch football tournament ceremony
With bottles of beer, bowls of fancy crisps,
Safe in our escapist bubble, for now.
Hope springs eternal that our team will win
Whilst in Palestine endless punishment
Persists.

Princes, prime ministers, presidents, clowns,
Carry on as if nothing has happened.
This ability to stand to one side,
To compartmentalise inside our brains
Such degradation of fellow humans,
Where does it come from? Is it genetic?
Are we all, to some degree, psychopaths?

Mainstream politicians polish their turds,
Spin webs of empty chocolate dipped words,
Applaud entrepreneurs new rocket ships,

JUXTAPOSITIONS

Another young sister gets blown to bits.
Earthlings, it seems, addicted to power,
Are happy to live in a world turned sour.
Reality depends on accidents
Of birth. Perspectives shaped by where we live.

Farage drives clapped out car from his garage,
Reverses into his own sick pothole,
Already occupied by Nazi pals.
Gaza appears once more upon our screens
Rafah explodes in afternoon heatwave,
Aid workers infinitely traumatised
Stare out at us as they plead for support.
You told me there is no alternative
To Keir Starmer and his Labour Party.
Surely there has to be a better way,
We all have to try and work something out.

16th June 2024.

66 - WHAT'S IT ALL FOR?

Forever war, forever more,
Is that what they fight for?
Put buildings up, knock buildings down
Is that what a town's for?
Lock protesters up in jail,
Is that what a law's for?
Spout propaganda all day long,
Is that what radio four's for?
Hospital wards filled to their brim,
What is NHS for?
Rishi Sunak pats his own back,
Is that what parliament's for?
Smarmy Starmer knifes his comrades,
Is that what Labour's for?
In Gaza more Yankee bombs fall,
Is that what we vote for?
Billionaires avoid their tax,
Is that what we pay for?
Farage and friends say what they like,
Is that what freedom's for?
Bent coppers get away with it,
Is that what Old Bill's for?
This year again we cast our votes,
What's democracy for?
Planet burns whilst tourists snuff it,
Tell me, What's it all for?
Hang on, England's just scored again,
Is THAT what it's all for?
Surely there's more to it than that?
Ain't there?
TELL ME,
AIN'T THERE?

19th June 2024

67 - WHAT BEAUTIFUL GAME?

Our future king wakes up in Germany,
Not so happy birthday for Prince of Wales,
Hopes now dashed of football hegemony,
Wind well and truly removed from their sails.

Gareth bemused as his tactics go South,
Shocked BBC pundits turn against team,
Shearer shouts loudest, turncoat motormouth,
It's a funny old game, know what I mean?

Passes continuously went astray,
Look for excuses, some blame state of pitch,
Whilst Marcus and Jack take forced holiday,
More tinkering now will not solve this glitch.

Millionaire players all took the piss,
Charlton Athletic play better than this.

21st June 2024

68 - ANNIBYNIAETH

You say that you want Palestine
To be an independent state.
So why not Cymru? Why not Wales?
You call it sectarian and tribal
To want to break away from royalty,
To leave subjugation from Westminster,
To want to be citizens not subjects?
It's neither sectarian nor tribal
To desire a free independent state,
Where people, who have never elected
A conservative government within
Its own borders, are constantly ruled
By a capitalist establishment,
Based in another country, miles away,
Achieve back its historic status.
This thirteenth century royalty theft,
On a par with common land enclosures,
Is grand imperialist larceny.
Long term British ruling class interests
Maintain this faux union with false laws.
You talk of socialism then stand
By whilst politicians chant crass anthems.
Sir Kier Starmer sings God Save The King,
Whilst draped in multiple union jacks,
Surrounded by hordes of Mandelsons hacks.
Freedom lies not through royal servitude,
But rather comes from repeatedly spoke truths
Found for all to see in annals of history.
United kingdom acts permanently
For benefit of unelected toffs.
Equality for all impossible
Within artificial democracy.
Cymru should stand tall amongst equals
ANNIBYNIAETH, ANNIBYNIAETH.

27th June 2024

69 - THIS GAME IS UP

It's too late for Rishi to score,
No bicycle kick will save him.
Goal posts have moved, bets have been placed,
Cleverly ain't face saver Kane.
Too many fans drifted away
Whilst king covid Boris partied.
True unaccountability
Queered pitches everywhere.
Cash transfers for contracts to friends,
Untendered, no competition.
Loudmouth Liz spouted growth, growth, growth,
All in all fourteen years of shite,
Where goals were missed, and strikers fouled.
No wonder, at last, this game is up.

2nd July 2024

70 - ELECTION REFLECTION

All those young greens
Watch old has beens
File back into Westminster,
Party machines
Destroy their dreams,
This world truly sinister.
Every sick vote
For stop the boats
Racist right from the get go.
Nigel Farage
Leaves his garage
Biggest liar we've met? No?
Maybe we're wrong,
Reform ain't strong,
Trumpism not over here.
Less people choose
To make the news
Don't cast their votes for Sir Keir,
Forty percent
Stayed in their tents
Turnout gets ever lower.
Landslide slips in,
Tories begin
Search for brand new BoJoer.
Watch as Lib Dems
Reborn again,
Storm backbencher seat tower,
A joke a day
What can one say?
One fun way to get power.
Our media
Ditches Gaza
Lets Israel off the hook,
Hides genocide,
Locks it inside
Closed pages of truth playbook.

6th July 2024.

71 - CAKEY BAKEY

I bought orange drizzle cake for Marley,
A spur of the moment thing.
Never thought about whether he'd like it,
Remember Grandad cake thing.
Turns out our young Marley's a bit cakey,
We got a cake thing going,
Maybe one day bake our own grandad cake,
We'll keep his knowledge growing.
Orange Grandad cake
Lemon Grandad cake
Limey Grandad cake
Berry Grandad cake
Nutty Grandad cake
Any Grandad cake
Let's make Grandad cake.
Sooner rather than later, Grandad cake,
Let's bake it with Marley, bake Grandad cake.

Grandad poem for Marley.

6th July 2024

72 - MINORITY MAJORITY

When almost twenty million don't vote
There is something wrong with democracy.
Low number voters put Keir Starmer in.
First passed the post unsatisfactory,
Each new minority majority
Keeps other minorities out.

Minority majority?
There has to be another way.
Minority majority?
Surely now this has had its day?

Inclusivity is put to one side,
I remember those words from H. G. Wells,
He said, "Every dogma has its day."
With FPTP it's become one way.
Exclusion of ideas destroys progress,
Encourages opportunists to bloom,
When we lock most people out closed doors will
Allow corporate fraud to bust and boom.

Minority majority?
There has to be another way.
Minority majority?
Surely now this has had its day?

Proportional representation NOW!

8th July 2024

73 - DIVE DEEPER INTO DEPTHS

Dog eat dog Tories turn on each other,
In public displays of desperation.
Who knows how many want to lead them now?
At this point, in our politics, who cares?

In opposition now there is no room
For fake Farage populist charisma.
Those who still stand witness extreme central
Control move exaltantly to power.

They recognise their own stupidity
When they allowed Johnson onto the Bridge
Only to crash into giant icebergs.
This is their Titanic moment writ large.

Suella conducts her dead orchestra,
As ruined ship plunges ever deeper.

11th July 2024

JUXTAPOSITIONS

74 - ARMS GROWTH X 3

The Lancet estimates death rates higher
Than at first thought in Gazan genocide.
Starmer and Biden begin new bromance,
All smiles and supportive White House statements.

Full military support for Ukraine,
No dicky birds for Palestinians,
They still remain persona non grata
For these two stalwart western arms traders.

New estimates say one in eight now dead,
Killed as a result of sick growth, growth, growth.
Obscene, murderous, rotten growth, growth, growth.
Arms companies red hot investables
For blood soaked capitalist assassins.

So ask yourself this question, did you vote
For parties that advocate growth, growth, growth?
Think hard about your answer if you did,
Because that might mean you are complicit.....

13th July 2024

75 - ANOTHER COLD SUMMER

It's another cold summer's morning,
A weak, pale yellow, sun shines wanly
Across West Wales frost spattered valley.
Kites whirl in their search for fresh carrion,
Buzzards, now depleted, still hunt rabbits.

On my radio news of an attempt
To assassinate Donald Trump rings out,
Nigel Farage makes crass one line statement,
He blames liberal anti Trump voices
For being horrible to his friend Don.

I go out and mow next door neighbour's lawn.
As I work air pressure changes, it's hot.
Beyond Teifi valley ominous clouds
Billow darkly across horizon hills.

Political foreboding fills my mind,
Spain win both Wimbledon and Euros cup.
A few black Cymru crows caw raucously,
It doesn't rain, clouds clear, bright half moon shines,
It's another cold summer's evening.

I go to my bed disturbed and quite sad.

13th July 2024.

76 - SUPERMARKET AMMO VENDING

Such normality of extremism
Worries all those who stand up and protest.
Liberals equated with psychopaths
By libertarian right wing racists,
On mainstream media, abetted by
Complicit journalists who daily smirk
At every opportunity to stick
Their corporate knives into left wing backs.

Clearly Trump's would be assassin was sick,
Psychologically disturbed product
Of a society obsessed with weapons.

Suddenly everyone seems to be shocked,
Whilst self service ammo machines open.

16th July 2024.

77 - DID YOU SEE?

Did you see? Did you see? Did you see him?
New foreign secretary shaking hands?
Shaking hand of a man who signed order
To drop those giant bunker buster bombs
On tented shelters full of homeless folk?

Did you see that photograph? Did you see?
Take a good look at Netanyahu's face.
He smiles broadly like a cat with fresh cream,
Two days after murdering innocents
In a so called designated safe zone.

Children decapitated as they played,
Limbs and body parts scattered far and wide.
Did…you….see….it? A propaganda coup
For annihilation in broadest daylight.

He shook his hand between furled up joint flags,
Picture that shows the world we support him.
I feel defiled by this obscenity.
This latest "landslide" is already dead.

17th July 2024.

JUXTAPOSITIONS

78 - CHEWING WASPS AT NIGHT.

Don't tell people what's going on
If you do you might get sent down.
New laws designed to smash protests
Will leave us chewing wasps at night.

Don't dare to speak truth to power,
Cometh wrong man, cometh lost hours.
Non violent direct action
Against agents of climate change?

Don't even think such thoughts today,
If you do don't vocalise them
Or else they'll bang you clean sway.
New ministers of thought check all
Contents of your chatrooms and Zooms.

Did we learn George Orwell's lessons?
Do we understand new newspeak?
Whilst we vote in new big brothers
Global warming hits higher peaks.

When there are no plants to forage,
When oceans have risen highest,
When London is under water,
No oats left to make our porridge,
Motorways have become useless,
All our best books are no good now
Nobody reads them anymore.

No-one articulates ideas
About how to change what we do,
It's too late, they've tied our tongues now,
Haven't they? Or maybe they ain't?
Can't lock all of us up. Can they?

20th July 2024.

79 - GOD SAVES WEIRDOS

Biden does a runner, Trump blows a fuse,
Only one sad old man left now to lose.
Media channels alive with known news,
Journalists scrabble for different views.

Soon Jeffrey Epstein's diary is published,
All hell breaks loose upon election trail,
Kamala updates vinyl collection,
Donald denies any recollection.

Meanwhile Joe's bombs keep carpeting Gaza,
Daily new podcasts ramp up fake tension,
MAGA memes explode, too many to mention,
Evangelicals hail their messiah,
J.D. pours petrol on rural bonfire.

Onwards and upwards this madness rolls on,
Come November which of them will be gone?

23rd July 2024

80 - WHERE JASMINE BLOOMS

Hot, sultry, overcast South London day.
Air hangs heavy beneath clouds, darkly grey.
Deptford and Greenwich reek of spilt sewage.
This trapped stench invades nostrils everywhere.

On corner of Vanguard and Friendly Street,
Perfume magnificently smells so sweet.
These myriad white flowers midst dark green
Makes me realise that even in foulest,
Stinkiest places nature provides hope.

Antidote to putrid Capitol shite.
Be thankful for relief that flows at night.
These days of climate warmed devastation
Changes how we smell centre of nation.

Luckily we have our wondrous Jasmine.

25th July 2024

81 - VIXEN IN DREAM VALE

She lay, as if asleep, amidst dried leaves,
Her head nestled against granite kerbstone.
This beautiful, noble, urban vixen
Stretched out in Morphius dream vale comfort,
Is quite dead beside parked up Lime hire e-bike.

I envy her perfect serenity
On this warm, late July, early evening.
For how long she'd been there we did not know,
There's no blood, but flies lay eggs as we look.
Bo and I head on for a beer, or two.

Strangely, after we leave The Brookmill pub,
Leaves and e-bike remain, but she is gone.
How or where just one more odd mystery,
In paradise, on streets of Deptford town.

26th July 2024

82 - DANCE PARTY?

Whatever has happened here?
Twenty yards on from Brookmill pub,
Small pile of shoes topped with clutch purse,
Arranged neat as a work of art.

Maybe a gutter dance party?
Some cool Deptford girls chased away
Whilst they whirled barefoot in circle?
Why didn't they come back again?

Or maybe someone has cleared out
Unwanted old accoutrements,
Emptied a small carrier bag
Surreptitiously late at night,
Too lazy to use refuse centre,
To make space in tiny wardrobe.

Whatever, it's normal round here,
South London streets a dumping ground.
People don't bother to fly tip
On green country sites anymore,
They just wander around corners,
Dump unwanted stuff, big or small,
And move on. Nobody cares less.

Whither street cleaning services?
Why don't Councils work anymore?
Is it down to austerity?
Who knows? Times changed since I lived here,
There's an air of fin de seicle.

Those shoes? That bag? No-one sees them.

24th July 2024.

83 - DAD AND ME

For three days my dad hid beneath a sheet
Of corrugated iron against wall
Whilst German troops swarmed throughout Nijmegen.
Cut off from his regiment, all alone,
A young musician in his mid twenties,

Trapped as war rages all across region.
Bombs dropped, shells burst, tanks rolled, morning, noon and night.
Eventually he did get away,
Swam across Waal river downstream from bridge.

He never spoke about his wartime days.
Spent his life buried in sheet music dreams.
His PTSD never left his mind,
Flared up when he watched film, "A Bridge Too Far."
He shook as he ran from that cinema.

I knew nothing of this until he died,
Explains why I couldn't reach him alive.

Such a shame, we could have been real good mates,
Dad and me. Took a lifetime to work out
How damaged he was by that bloody war.

July 30th 2024

84 - AT OUR GATE

These nazis always spread fear of others,
It's how fascists work between their covers.
Bigger is better when it comes to lies,
Media hacks rehearse their alibis.

For years headlines screamed "We Must Stop The Boats",
Even New Labour thought that would win votes.
Elon's pet plaything, now burning red hot,
With Trump like fake news algorithmic bots.

Politics feels a little bit dirty,
We have segued back to nineteen thirty.
Far right extremists attack police cars,
Will Suella's laws put them behind bars?

Riled up barbarians stand at our gate,
If we don't stand firm will it be too late?

1st August 2024.

JUXTAPOSITIONS

85 - TIME IS OF THE ESSENCE

The current narrative that is being propounded by the MSM is one which suggests that there are flying right wing activists moving around the country and launching these riots on the streets of Britain. This is too simplistic an analysis. This situation cannot ignore some key points about how we have arrived at this scenario. These are, in no particular order, in my view, as follows:-

- The use of social media by the likes of Yaxley Lennon, Farage, Trump and others is dangerous and has been allowed to grow by the billionaire oligarchs such as Elon Musk in the misguided name of Freedom. As R H Tawney said in 1931 in his book Equality "Freedom for the pike is death to the minnow.". Twitter, Telegram and Tik-Tok are being used very effectively to build networks that do not need people to travel vast distances to attend their riots.

- It is clear that the neo-liberal political consensus that has existed since the election of Margaret Thatcher in 1979 has reached a nadir in terms of support from the British electorate, this is highlighted by the fact that over 40% didn't vote in the last election. That can only be because people have not seen any major policies to deal with the large scale problems brought about by the onset of the post industrial society. Large swathes of the population feel disenfranchised because of the failure to provide adequate economic development, affordable housing, decent health and social care. The people no longer trust the mainstream political parties to act in their interests hence the four and a half million votes garnered by Farage and Reform.

- The Labour Party have failed to understand the deep consequences of implementing austerity policies whilst at the same time colluding with the growth, growth, growth, policies of the super rich. The Corbyn experiment failed for a number of reasons, mainly, in my opinion, the belief that the fabled broad church actually existed within the party as whole and that the Parliamentary Labour Party members would follow the wishes of the party membership via conference policy making decisions. The PLP didn't, and this was why Labour failed to win the 2017 GE. On top of this the Corbyn team also failed to deal with the constitutional and administrative structures put in place during the Kinnock/Blair years which led to absolute disaster that was the 2019 election campaign. Now we see the consequences with the election of what can only be described as a car-crash for socialism.

- So, if ever there was a time for a broad based coalition of the left to form a true opposition to both the far right who are organising riots on the streets, and the neo-liberals in the House of Commons and The Senedd, it is now. Clearly Starmer, Reeves and Cooper are going to use the Police to try and smash the far right. This is fraught with danger in my view for all the reasons above and more. There needs to be a complete transitional change of direction towards ensuring that there is a future for the working class in Britain. Without that the doors to power are left open to the fascists. There are various groups of socialists, green activists, anarchists and others talking about how to bring about an alternative to the failed policies of the mainstream parties. I urge all of us involved in this process to recognise the urgency of the situation and put aside ideological differences to finally build the coalition that some of us have been calling for for many many years.

4th August 2024

86 - FIRST JOB

I ruled red lines on deeds
Beneath important words
Names and places in caps.

Contracts and agreements
Last wills and testaments
Each day bored me to sleep,
I'd collapse across desk,
Pen and ruler in hand.

With my head full of song
Drifted into dreamland.
It was pure Xanadu,
Back then I never knew
That I'd gone through a door.

Should have written it down
But I was paid to work.
Old Fred would wake me up,
Shake me from reverie,
That place beside boredom
Called imagination.

Some years on I got it,
Now, through my half closed eyes,
I see things more clearly,
In nineteen sixty two
My first job was crappy.

At least, at last, I know.

11th August 2024

JUXTAPOSITIONS

87 - A BREAK IN FOG OF WAR

On high edge of Hinterland above Borth
Look across coastal path to Irish Sea.
Sun shines after misty clouds blow away,
I read three poems aloud al fresco.

It's a perfect end to our barbecue,
New friendships formed, forward action plans forged.
Sheep are herded into another field
Whilst children whoop and run around freely.

This perfect bucolic Celtic idyll
Is what we need to maintain sanity
In a world driven beyond humanity.

In car on way home radio broadcasts
Latest Israeli atrocity.
This fog of war rolls relentlessly on.

11th August 2024.

JUXTAPOSITIONS

88 - STATEHOOD NOW

You don't want to hear this,
I'll tell you anyway.
In your paranoia
Find seeds of fascism.
You verify your truth
With opposite visions
Of what is going on.

Leaflets flutter from sky,
Not everyone sees them,
Some manage to get out
From yesterday's safe zone,
Shuffled back onto road
For umpteenth time in fear.
One more bunker bomb dropped
On school sanctuary.

This is your gold standard
Of civilian care,
Disintegrated kids
Mixed into bomb rubble.
You attack journalists
For spread of false stories
Whilst you deny access.

Your propaganda filled
With worst of distortion,
No thought of proportion.
Within your twisted mind
All Palestinians,
Bar none, are terrorists.

You justify murder
Of innocent children
In relentless pursuit
Of an endless pogrom
With historic echoes.
Your care filled handiwork
Indiscriminately
Destroys municipal
Buildings willy nilly.

JUXTAPOSITIONS

Public services gone,
Businesses are flattened,
Wrecked houses bulldozed,
Sewage system destroyed.
You brazenly talk of
Public Relations war,
Your sick echo chamber
Perpetuates revenge
In terms we recognise.

You say they want to die
In order to gain more
Support from outside world.
Can't believe you said that.
I listen close again,
I am flabbergasted.
Illegal collective
Punishment eludes you,
You view all as guilty.

In Gaza, In West Bank,
Wherever you find them,
Human collateral
To be ever damaged
For their freedom demands.

You paint yourself further
Into bigot's corner
There complain forever
That you are a victim.
Your gaslight fades daily
As we see straight through it.

All we want to see is
Statehood for Palestine.

14th August 2024

89 - STOP GO STOP GO

Stop go Stop go
Red Green Red Green
Instigators
Are all about

Stop go Stop go
Red Green Red Green
Instigators
Join us and shout

Stop go Stop go
Stop go Stop go
There's a need to make a change
Red Green Red Green
Red Green Red Green
A real need to rearrange

Instigate change
Instigate change
Help us change our world today

Stop Go Red Green
Stop Go Red Green
Instigate real change today

Over Under Upside Down
Side by Side and Inside Out
Red Green Red Green
Stop Go Stop Go
Instigators come on out

Instigators Come On Out
Instigators Stand and Shout
Red Green Red Green
Stop Go Stop Go

Harry Rogers 16th August 2024

90 - GLOBAL CHILDCARE

When all children are hungry we feed them.
When all children cry we have to hug them.
All young children learn when we teach them.
When all children are ill we nurture them.

Don't we? Don't we? Perhaps sometimes we do,
Mostly we're too busy with our arms fairs,
We crave profits from wars, more growth, growth, growth.
Childhood innocence way down agenda.

Psychopathic war lords dictate futures,
Economic stability relies
On continuous export of weapons
Used to regularly bomb fake safe zones.

Human beings are obsessed with conflict,
As yet, nowhere near civilisation.

17th August 2024.

JUXTAPOSITIONS

91 - BREAKAWAY

Kier Starmer says nothing of any worth
To those who suffer illegal war crimes.
Mainstream media have it covered though,
Today on Radio four they discussed
Whether our prime minister's entitled
To breakaway on summer holiday.

Well? Is he? Entitled to breakaways?
Can he jet off to an oligarch's pad?
In Italy, just like Tony Blair did?
Nip out to Heathrow, fly off to a beach?
Take a couple of red boxes with him?
After all, gotta keep abreast of things.

No breakaways for people in Gaza,
No airport in occupied Palestine.

18th August 2024.

92 - PUBLIC CASH COWS

Labour or Tory, whichever which way,
Austerity is still Austerity.
From services now too cash strapped to care
Last drops of blood are squeezed by auditors.

After fifty plus years of those three Es
Effective, efficient, economic,
Put in place by Thatcherite accountants
Who cared nothing for our society.

Health, education, housing, and transport,
All become capitalist cash cows.
Neo liberal Randian nightmares
Now accepted as modern new normal.

Faux democracy enables this farce
Labour or Tory two cheeks of same arse.

19th August 2024.

93 - BANG 'EM ALL AWAY

Bang 'em up, Bang 'em up,
Bang 'em all away.
Send them all to chokey
Those rioters and thugs
Prison's a deterrent
That ought to be enough.
Bang 'em up, Bang 'em up,
Bang 'em all away.

Worked out well that last time,
Never mind politics,
Nor any reasons why,
We'll focus on their crimes.
Bang 'em up, Bang 'em up,
Bang 'em all away.

Let's pass some brand new laws,
Give police more powers
Smash up all disorder
Don't ask nor question WHY?
Bang 'em up, Bang 'em up,
Bang 'em all away.

Let racism fester,
It's too hard to deal with,
Because it's everywhere,
Even in New Labour.
Bang 'em up, Bang 'em up,
Bang 'em all away.

When they're all in prison
Then what shall we do?
When we've run out of cells?
Erm I dunno. Do you?

Harry Rogers, 20th August 2024.

JUXTAPOSITIONS

94 - DIVERSIONARY DOWNBURST

Billionaire's super yacht sinks off Sicily,
Why is every news channel so obsessed by this?
Ships sink each week on a global basis.
What's so special about this tragedy?

News media swamped daily by coverage
Of a small, sad, shipwreck catastrophe,
Whilst in Gaza strip and on The West Bank,
Genocide continues unabated
With hardly any reportage for days.
News hacks trot out lines about ceasefire talks
That American government desires
In order to demonstrate some control
Over global events in election year.

Netanyahu doesn't listen to them,
He needs his fix of war fueled oxygen
To maintain personal hegemony.
Once conflict is ended he's a dead duck.
Bombs drop, bullets fly, houses fall, kids die,
Famine, disease and sickness grow daily,
Meanwhile headlines focus on super yacht,
Waterspout or downburst? Something is weird.

Such overt diversion of attention
Away from this gigantic, putrid, stain
On human history is disgraceful.
Press editors should hang their heads in shame,
So should our politicians in power.

25th August 2024.

95 - TEENAGE BEATNIK SUMMER

When Angel John lent me his On The Road
By Jack Kerouac I was just fourteen.
When I read that in nineteen sixty two
It changed my life forever and a day.

For a while I mooched round like a beatnik,
Listened to jazz, blues and Françoise Hardy,
Wore a dark blue duffle jacket and shades.
Angel John and I hung in coffee bars,
Smoked Disque Bleu cigarettes, we were cool.

At fifteen we flew away to Paris,
Rented a small room on Isle St Louis,
We saw Willie Dixon and Memphis Slim
Sing Pigalle Love live aux Trois Mailletz.
A beautiful teenage beatnik summer.

26th August 2024

96 - GOOD OL' DAYS?

Soon there'll be no-one left who remembers
How we all played cowboys and indians,
Hidden in bracken on London bomb sites,
In nineteen fifties, with our bamboo bows.

When a few farthings felt like a fortune,
Wolverhampton Wanderers exotic,
Jerry Lee Lewis outraged everyone.
I read my young brother to sleep each night
With stories of Dan Dare and Marvel Man.

Things weren't all good though in post war Britain,
Polio still crippled many children,
Everybody smoked fags until they died,
Wages were low, and racism flourished.
I got told off 'cos I played in our street
With Jamaican kids when first they arrived.

Seventy years on prejudice still
Abounds, fueled by Nazi fear of other.
Mostly though life's better than "good ol" days",
Apart from climate change etcetera......

26th August 2024

97 - LOOK FORWARD IN ANGER

All of those rotten red tory boroughs
That run our services into buffers
Offer their allegiance to Rachel Reeves
Make life a misery for those in need.

They say they have to fix foundations
Gloss over pensioner protestations.
Starmer stands tough in Downing Street garden,
Tells us all times are about to harden.

Things will get worse before they get better,
October budget poison pen letter,
Blames last government for all of our pain,
Ordinary people pay costs again.

Elsewhere Oasis spread opium new,
Extort half billion from me and you.

27th August 2024

JUXTAPOSITIONS

98 - NOUVEAU COLONIALISM

New colonials from old colonies
Want to colonise those smashed up remains
Left behind along what we called Gaza Strip
By Israel Defence Force murder squad.

Demolition and eradication
Of all traces of Palestinians
Are ultimate aims of Zionist cult
To allow nouveau colonisation.

Already cultural centres are gone,
Universities, and schools, destroyed,
State terrorism by occupiers,
Relentlessly inflicted for ten months
Whilst artificial ceasefire talks roll on,
Nothing but a colonial land grab.

28th August 2024

JUXTAPOSITIONS

99 - BIRD FREE ZONES

Their handcuffs are too tight,
Both her hands are turned blue
They will not loosen them,
She's asked, but they won't.
They slowly trash her home
In their balaclavas,
Gather up every bit
Of electrical kit.

Computers, microphones,
Address books, telephones,
She can't communicate.
One more gagged journalist,
Stopped from doing her work.
It feels so Kafkaesque
As she watches home smashed
By counter terrorist
Squad in balaclavas.

Her dead mothers ashes
Tipped from urn and scattered
Willy nilly across
Attic floor as they search
For what they will not say.
Now under house arrest,
Her travel rights denied,
She can no longer stand
Up strong for Palestine,
No more to speak her truths,
Trapped in Orwellian
Nightmare by government
Dictat under orders
From New Labour office
Of Home Secretary,
Yvette Cooper MP.

Modern democracy
Under first past the post,
A Landslide victory,
Where they can, and will, do
Anything they want to

JUXTAPOSITIONS

Just to get their own way.

While still bombs drop, drones fly,
Tanks roll, spies spy, kids die,
Mainstream media lies,
Genocide makes us cry.

2nd September 2024

JUXTAPOSITIONS

100 - SWALLOWS

Swallows noisily swoop and dive
Through an insect filled gloaming haze,
These halcyon summers end days
Soon over when they fly away.

Fewer now than olden days past.
If we could make golden days last,
Such times as these engraved on hearts,
We would, of course, but it feels late,
I watch four horses pass our gate.

Still I feel it is my duty
To document fleeting beauty.
I sit, still, quiet as a mouse,
Watch magic birds wheel round our house.
Trees begin turn to red and gold,
How lucky to see this unfold.

Such moments rare in modern times
As change roars on across all climes.

4th September 2024

JUXTAPOSITIONS

101 - DEAD OPPOSITION?

Things can only get worse, so says Starmer.
He means it. These are very scary times.
Technically Labour has a mandate,
Even though forty percent did not vote.

More people abstained than voted Labour.
Democracy rapidly suffocates,
Drowned by neo liberals on fake stilts.
Poets, journalists and academics
Face gagged futures if they dare write truth.

Bots, crawlers, algorithms and cookies
Infect all our internet connections.
Freedom of communication hijacked
By rogue billionaire chaos mongers
Who milk their shedloads from all and sundry.

IT revolution is now become
A maelstrom of lies writ by fascist shills.
All positive aspects slowly wiped out
Gradually there's no opposition
As we are led to view state lies as truth
By party hacks who ignore need for proof.

All of us now must hail shibboleths
Drawn up to glorify extreme centre.
Protesters against Gazan genocide
Now identified as crude terrorists.

Things have already gotten a lot worse.
I ask myself how much worse can things get?

Harry Rogers, 5th September 2024.

102 - FREE LIKE A SWALLOW

Nothing is quite as sleek as swallow flight.
Watched in awe as one swooped across my field,
Feeding on insects above new mown hay.
Such beauty in low slung sunset evening.

That night I drift quickly into a dream,
I'm in flight above Andalusia.
Mediterranean sea glints below.
By my side flies swallow I watched today.

It turns its head towards me, winks an eye,
Then swoops low over beach at La Linea.
I follow, late October sun warms back,
There are hundreds of us, all together.

I have wings,
I can fly,
I am free,
Like Swallows.

Somehow, I know exactly what to do,
We glide on across Straits of Gibraltar,
Towards mountains of Western Morocco.
I have never felt such freedom as this.

It feels so real to be up with swallows
As they head home away from our winter.
I wake when a sunbeam plays on my face,
But my mind is still in that airborne space.

I need wings
For to fly
To be free
Like swallows

9th September 2024.

JUXTAPOSITIONS

103 - ON DYFED LAN Y MÔR

Ancient greyed singlets and long Johns
Flutter casually in breeze
So gently blown from Sahara
To warm these Teifi Valley hills.

It's September, summer's over,
Camper vans leave resorts in droves,
Local dogs bounce on Poppit Sands,
Fairweather sailors batten down,
Cliffe golfers lose last seabound balls.

Canada geese in vee shape squawk
High above Cardigan Island.
Such days on Dyfed Lan Y Môr,
Where kites fly and Seagulls hover,
Curlews sing from sand dunes afar,
Carparks emptied, cafes closed up,
Herald freedom of open space,
From beach bound tourists all gone home.

These are our true halcyon days.

9th September 2024.

JUXTAPOSITIONS

104 - TUNNELS END

Difficult choices
We all have to make
Different voices
Some of them are fake
Prison releases
Set them free early
Iron out creases
Straightened or curly
Winter fuel payments
Mostly strip away
Safe fiscal raiments
Bills too high to pay
Poetic volleys
Salvos of bold words
Old centrist wallys
Spew out cruel turds
National renewal,
Face stormy weather,
Private and public,
All in together.
Cheers for new fears dear,
Life only gets worse,
You've got a nerve Keir,
Rob pensioner's purse.
End opposition,
Protest off our streets,
Activist prisons,
New Labour sweet treats.
Watch extreme centre
As they blow their tops,
Things won't get better,
Till all this shit stops.
Tell not again of
Light end of tunnel
As we head towards
Cremation funnel.

11th September 2024

105 - PULL UP MY DUVET

When nuclear potentiality
Turns into global actuality
There's no return from our stupidity,
Nor our love affair with cupidity.

Celebrities suddenly discover
How to abuse religiosity,
Embrace prophecies as they recover
From modern fortune driven pomposity.

Priesthoods depicted gods as supermen,
Reversed by uber riche upstart godheads.
World stage creaks with their animosity,
We suffer arrogant hypocrisy.

Gooners gurn in private directors box,
War factory chimneys belch monkey pox,
Pensioners told we must be practical,
Putin threatens nuclear, tactical.

Fuck all their flags and their fucking borders,
Fuck all neo-liberal marauders,
I pull my duvet up over my head,
Today I think, perhaps, I'll stay in bed.

23rd September 2024.

JUXTAPOSITIONS

106 - WE WILL WHEN YOU WON'T!!!

We will if you won't
We will if you don't
Protest against war
We will when you won't

You say your party
Your Labour Party
Your party has changed
New Labour Party

What is it all for?
Your Labour Party.
Don't mention this war
Sick Labour Party

She said you're no longer
A party of protest.
Then what are you there for
If never to protest?

Kier's speech was a car crash
He don't know his onions
Served bangers without mash
No word of his cash stash

They jeer from their lecturn
At protest whilst kids burn
Is this what it's all for?
A jamboree star turn?

Points finger at racists,
Gets standing ovation,
Keeps lid on Forde report,
This hypocrite leader.

You say your party
Your Labour Party
Your party has changed
New Labour Party

JUXTAPOSITIONS

What is it all for?
Your Labour Party.
Don't mention this war
Sick Labour Party

We will if you won't
We will if you don't
Protest against war
We will when you won't

24th September 2024

JUXTAPOSITIONS

107 - CURVES

Learning curves grow steeper with each new year,
Soon we'll all become software engineers.
We've forgotten all about MS DOS,
Word Perfect, Napster and all that other dross.

Old silver surfers ride third waves online,
Our communications get there on time.
Still inquisitive after all these years,
We've learned, that hard way, to conquer our fears.

Now we use our phones to pay for our beers,
Suddenly discover cash disappears.
Freedoms salami sliced, till we're bereft,
I T stole them all, soon there's nothing left.

Social media moulds conversations,
Wars continue to decimate nations.
Beep beep, Hello? It's another cold call,
We tell them Sod off, then give them fuck all.

Inside echo chambers people relax,
Trolls sniff around whilst they gather up facts,
Confidence tricksters continue to steal,
And now, in A.I. world, nothing is real.

Harry Rogers 26th September 2024

108 - SUNSET DREAM TIME

Red Cats dance in sunset dream light,
On inlet beach at end of days.

Soon such visions will be long gone,
Temperature hits fifty five,
No human beings left alive,
No more antics from crazy cats,
Nor wistful howls from lonesome dogs,
Nobody smells vast forest fires,
Cars move not in flooded cities,
A I has failed to save our souls.
Still, we make most of beauty now,
We'll dance with sand between our toes,
With all those other crazy cats.

How long we've got? Nobody knows,
But sunset dream time grows, and grows.

3rd October 2024.

JUXTAPOSITIONS

109 - I WANT TO IGNORE

How hard do I want to ignore B J,
Not have to deal with this clown day by day,
Now back on our screens thanks to Laura K,
I wish that he would fuck off clean away.

He's written a new book so pundits say,
Unleashed where he can let his mantras play,
Signed copies one hundred pounds, who will pay?

He still sees himself a roaring success,
Whilst most of us pay to clear up his mess,
Arrogance means he will never confess.

He never swallows his own bitter pill,
Perhaps this joker is mentally ill.

4th October 2024.

110 - FIGHT FOR TRUTH?

BBC news tells us they fight for truth
Use video links to demonstrate proof,
Their journalists visit all world hot spots
Make us believe they're all total hot shots.

Most of these old hacks are now broken down,
Editors shred their work, they look like clowns,
Fuel obsession with both sides of story,
Lack of proportion, leader a Tory.

Genocide mongers given space to spout,
Is this what licence fees are all about?
Every year since nineteen forty eight
Support Israeli love affair with hate.

Tell us now which side is armed to their teeth?
Why does our media support a thief?

5th October 2024.

111 - NO EXIT

Where there's no escape there ain't any hope.
In Gaza there are no travel agents,
No routes out to freedom, no rail stations,
Nor any airport departure lounges,
No Mediterranean ferry ports,
It's impossible to leave anymore.
We all know this as we watch from afar.
Occupiers come and go as they please,
Occupied are bombed daily to their knees,
Bulldozers pass shell shocked child amputees,
We ready ourselves for next Halloween.
Can anything get to be more obscene?
Genocide immersed on our smart phone screens,
Justice less likely than it's ever been.

9th October 2024.

112 - SAIL ON

I drive along Emlyn High Street
One sunny Friday afternoon,
See Derek, my old sailor friend,
Sail along in electric chair,
Cigarette in hand, wind in hair.

Minus his legs, large grin on face,
Don't know how, but he's made me smile,
As he did when we moored off Dale.

9th October 2024

113 - WHAT A STATE WE'RE IN

Our democracy is problematic,
Our democracy ain't democratic,
All this time we've had state ochlocracy,
There's something wrong with our democracy.

Unelected yobs rule our polity,
Hidden behind fake rules and policies,
Every few years we choose without choices,
From crass unrepresentative voices.

All this time we've got aristocracy,
A state mafia that robs you and me,
Where children are born to be kings and queens,
Unprivileged cast off as never beens.

Power without responsibility
Keeps royal heads safe beneath golden crowns,
No-one from inside our vast majority
Walks out upon this stolen hallowed ground.

Jet off to Davos, all these high fliers,
Maintain status quo, corporate liars,
Arms factory chimneys belch constant smoke,
Whilst global warming is tret as a joke.

All of us powerless, that's you and me,
Do as we're told for false economy,
Listen with care as they trot out their oath,
All will be well when they increase new growth.

But we all know what happens when they don't
Reach their targets, as we know that they won't,
Austerity floodgates open again,
Poverty struck people absorb most pain.

Salami slice cuts to balance their books,
Make new fiscal rules, who cares how it looks?
Main thing that matters, hour by hour,
Elites ensure they hang on to power.

JUXTAPOSITIONS

They claim a landslide, we know it ain't true,
Forty percent never voted. Did you?
New Labour government, victorious,
Twenty percent support ain't glorious.

At despatch box, in emperor's new clothes,
Out of his depth now 'cos everyone knows
Our democracy is problematic,
Our democracy ain't democratic.

9th October 2024

JUXTAPOSITIONS

114 - FLY AWAY RONNIE O'

I hear Ronnie O' on my radio
He works it all out on my radio
Casts himself away on my radio
Remembers his dad on my radio

Fly away
Ronnie O'
Fly away
Ronnie O'
Anywhere
Fly away
Ronnie O'
Fly away

All his addictions on my radio
Laid out clean and bare on my radio
He seems in control on my radio
Escapes in his life on my radio

Fly away
Ronnie O'
Fly away
Ronnie O'
Anywhere
Fly away
Ronnie O'
Fly away

Talks of dot paintings on my radio,
Runs and runs and runs on my radio,
Paint your dots then pot your shots Ronnie O'
Think on, how lucky you are Ronnie O'.

10th October 2024.

115 - REPUBLICAN BLUES

Whilst fruits of our labour rot in their banks,
They loan out money for missiles and tanks,
Fly them to Israel for use in war,
Such horror for decades, what's it all for?

Trump and Musk spin fast like wild tornados,
Bigger lies daily, insanity grows,
Two ego trippers whirl madly on stump,
Elon tries hard to out trump Donald Trump.

How do Americans swallow their pill?
Clearly their empire's seriously ill,
Disruption's so "modern", it's all the go,
Bamboozle people with things they don't know.

God help us all whether they win or lose,
By winter we'll have Republican blues.

12th October 2024.

JUXTAPOSITIONS

116 - GOLF IN GWBERT

I mine my past for those sweet memories,
When I wasn't lonely, inside my dreams.
I spend more time alone now that I'm old,
But at least I am warm, which is positive.

Tomorrow play golf at Cliffe Hotel
This tricky course that I know very well.
Balls will fly into Teifi estuary,
Or disappear into hideous rough.

Wind will create havoc with shots galore
But I will not care, this is half our fun,
Afterwards? Lunch with friend at nineteenth hole.

We'll talk politics, music, and health news,
On such days old geezers come back to life,
One can but hope that a bright sun will shine.

14th October 2024

JUXTAPOSITIONS

117 - WHAT'S ON T.V. THIS EVENING?

When there's nowhere to go back to, then what?
Construct shantys around public buildings,
Try hard to overcome paranoia
Alongside frightened and harassed neighbours,
Wait patiently for inevitable.

Eventually bombs explode gas bottles,
Fires rage and set light to children in bed.
They run on fire to their freaked out parents.
Global television carries images
Of nightly atrocities in Gaza.

We watch whilst we eat our evening dinner,
Drink an after-work glass of wine or beer,
Appalled by ubiquitous violence,
Whilst we scroll channels for entertainment.

14th October 2024

JUXTAPOSITIONS

118 - OYSTERS GRIT AND PEARLS

Oysters, Grit and Pearls
Oysters, Grit and Pearls
If we want a better world
Oysters, Grit and Pearls

When we sit in cozy rooms with our friends,
We know that there are lots of things to change.
We also know this pain will never end
Until we buck their trend.

While we ossify and never make change,
We know nothing will ever rearrange,
If nobody disrupts our status quo
No future dreams will grow.

Oysters, Grit and Pearls
Oysters, Grit and Pearls
If we want a better world
Oysters, Grit and Pearls

If we live in oyster shells without grit
All we'll ever get is that same old shit
If we ain't got grit in our oyster shell
We'll never make a pearl.

Sometimes in life we need to disagree,
We have to shout for peace and dignity,
Sometimes there just ain't nothing else for it,
We all have to be grit,

Oysters, Grit and Pearls
Oysters, Grit and Pearls
If we want a better world
Oysters, Grit and Pearls

Harry Rogers, 16th October 2024.

119 - CAST OFF COMFORT

Beware those echo chambers
Filled up with shared ideas that
Run forever as whispers
Around and around their well
Worn gallery overcoats.

Those overcoats that are so
Comfortable and friendly
That it's easy to believe
That, because they feel so snug,
All is well in our wider world.

We know full well that it ain't.

Harry Rogers, 19th October 2024

JUXTAPOSITIONS

120 - WHAT A SPECIES!

Time stands still, all is destroyed,
Nothing changes, nothing's left.
Unmanned aerial vehicles
Have a supreme relevance
To carnage in Palestine.

Modern weapons are obscene,
None more so than unmanned drones.
Very few people spoke out
Against National Assembly
When they attempted to set up
A centre of excellence
For UAVs in West Wales
As part of Labour Party
Economic Development
Plans to bring jobs to what was
Europes poorest region.

Even Labour leftie doyen,
Diane Abbott saw drones as
Just another war weapon,
Legitimate part of defence.
Some of us tried to warn them
About autonomy.
Back then nobody listened,
Our MPs failed to understand.

Now it's way too late to
Put genies back in bottles,
Or chicks back into egg shells.
Now robots film human death
Whilst media show videos.
Edited war propaganda
Floods all mainstream news programme screens.

Israel bans all journalists
Exerts control of imagery.
Surveillance linked A I programmes,
Developed in Parc Aberporth,
Built into Watchkeeper snoop drones,

JUXTAPOSITIONS

Autonomously choose targets.
It's a win win situation.

Expensive troop numbers cut back,
Fewer soldiers in body bags,
Drones far cheaper than fighter jets,
Dollars, Shekels, Euros and Pounds,
Modern warfare cheaper all round.
Majority of victims now
Civilians caught in between,
Collateral cannon fodder,
Dehumanised, expendable,
Ultimately forgettable.

Soon enough news becomes movies,
Military industrialists
Bank cash, same as they ever did.
This dystopia is far worse
Than any pulp sci-fi novel.
What kind of world do we live in
Where our taxes fuel genocide,
Senior politicians lie
Daily as a matter of course.

New Draconian laws are passed,
Old fashioned protests from our past
Impossible now. Freedom dies
As we play war games on our phones,
In brave new world of unmanned drones,
Something incredible's happened.

Homo Sapiens eh?

What a species!

Harry Rogers, 20th October 2024.

121 - NOUVEAU DEATH EMPIRE

With those things you thought so scary
Far, far behind you in your past,
Ain't much time to be full of fear,
Welcome to nouveau death empire.

But what of this mess we have left behind?
Where are those answers that we could not find?
Storms rage, ever harder, day after day,
Birds and butterflies now withered away,
We remember that war to end all wars,
It carries on behind different doors.
Now, eyes open to realisation,
There's no such thing as civilisation.
All politicians play hard these charades,
To maintain power for those who hold cards,
Everyone else now can go to a wall,
To be gunned down because they mean fuck all.

Taken a lifetime to get here,
Can't believe we made it this far,
Almost at end of eighth decade,
Realise how lucky we are.
We're no longer frightened by fire,
Welcome to nouveau death empire.

21st October 2024

122 - HASS GEBIERT KRIEG

Käthe Kollwitz held her mirror firmly,
She thought she was revolutionary,
Then found she was evolutionary.
Her works against war speak louder each day.

She understood how one war breeds next war.
We see future war seeds scattered daily
From banks nurtured by capitalist growers,
Thrown left and right by nationalist sowers,
From skies above Gaza and Lebanon.

We're told a ceasefire may be possible,
As death and destruction trundle onwards.
Peacetalks are evermore illusory.

Watch as London, Washington and Berlin
Commit support for war never ending.

21st October 2024

JUXTAPOSITIONS

123 - UBIQUITY OF MONSTERS

As Gramsci's postwar monsters multiply
Our shite media sculpts our perception.
Propagandists have replaced journalists
As an Orwellian nightmare shines bright.

How casual is acceptance portrayed
Of justified genocide day and night.
An IDF spokesman shrugs his shoulders,
When questioned about destruction of homes
With people inside now dead and buried.

"This is war.", he says. Hamas defeated.
But they won't stop until surrender comes.
We watch occupiers shoot occupied
As if they're on a stall at Blackheath Fair,
Gramsci's right, monsters ubiquitous.

22nd October 2024

124 - IN QUIET SPACE

On a sunny day I find a quiet space,
Where I can sit and write my poetry.
Thoughts flow easily beside our Acer,
Nature spurs me onward through angry world.

I fight back heady guilt filled emotions
About how lucky I am to sit here,
Inside this bucolic Celtic idyll,
Whilst comrades are slaughtered in Palestine.

Sunshine and birdsong enchant my senses
But I am constantly drawn to fences
That need to be pulled down in freedom's name.

At my vast age all I can do is sit
In my garden sanctuary and write,
I have to write, no matter this beauty.

Harry Rogers 23rd October 2024

JUXTAPOSITIONS

125 - BEYOND DYSTOPIA

There are places on Earth that have become
Beyond dystopia, beyond reason.
Gaza is number one on current list,
Israel smashes down an iron fist.

Sodden with blood, of innocent victims,
Their spokespeople are unbelievable
In their pursuit of eradication,
Destruction, through collective punishment.

Genocide, one step beyond dystopia,
Denied daily across "news" platforms.
This crass focus on a right to defend
Absolutely beyond acceptable.

Our Prime Minister, disgrace in power,
Makes us all complicit in this bloodbath.
Four fifths of our electorate did not
Vote for naked abuse of reality.

We demand unconditional ceasefire,
NOW!!!

26th October 2024.

126 - DREAM OR NIGHTMARE?

I don't understand why America
Believes it's own omnipotent story.
Why must every other country bow down
To power addicts of former glory?

MAGA maniacs enact their own memes,
Invest lives in destructive nihilist schemes,
Believe cranky unbelievable dreams,
History rewritten, or so it seems.

Democracy twitches in Trump's gutter,
Outrageous statements his bread and butter.
Ghosts who fought Nazis are all a splutter,
Hitler was good, says this fascist nutter.

We're one week away from total mayhem,
Ballots mean nothing to mad supermen.

28th October 2024

JUXTAPOSITIONS

127 - TERROR?

Who is a terrorist?
A dead girl with a bullet in her skull?
Was she a terrorist?
Headless boy with no legs?
Was he a terrorist?
Dead mother, hole in breast?
Was she a terrorist?
Grandad beneath rubble?
Was he a terrorist?
Is every smashed up corpse a terrorist?
Those random refugees shot in their streets?
Are they all terrorists?
Those vaporised bunker bombed grandmothers?
Were they the terrorists?
Collectively punished burnt school teachers?
Were they the terrorists?
All Palestinian civilians?
All of them? Terrorists?

A sick mass collective paranoia
Grips state occupiers.
These purveyors of modern genocide?
Perhaps they're terrorists?
Terrorism spreads, morning, noon, and night,
But innocents aren't terrorists, are they?
When will humanity end all terror?

I saw a girl with a hole in her head,
Her blood runs across Gazan cobblestones,
Now I feel more terrified than ever.

2nd November 2024

128 - COMPLICITY CONTINUITY

Continuity of complicity
Is pretty much a foregone conclusion.
Now Badenoch is new Tory leader,
Parliament maintains shite illusion.

Starmer with fake landslide majority
Will struggle to avoid mass confusion,
Spread wide largely of his own volition.
Voters suffered multiple delusions,
Despite a landslide, there is no mandate,
Two fifths stayed at home, in their seclusion.

Labour won as Farage split Tories votes,
With large pseudo Trumpian allusions.
Now all our MPs discuss exclusion,
I dread a massive fascist transfusion.

4th November 2024

JUXTAPOSITIONS

129 - TRICKS OR TREATS?

Are they mad?
Do they like boot flavours?
They must do, given how many times their
Feet go into their mouths.

Increase public transport fares,
But hold fuel prices down?
Surely these are actions of a first class clown.
Spend billions on Trident replacement,
Whilst they bleat on about massive black hole.

They trot out failed ex MP on Newsnight,
She lays blame on careless last government,
Prattles on about our security.

This budget, hard to call,
Backs firmly against wall,
Rob Peter, don't pay Paul,
Watch on as mighty fall.

Trick us or treat us, we all need to know,
Time has run away, which way will things go?

4th November 2024

JUXTAPOSITIONS

130 - WALL STREET WINS AGAIN

There's only one winner in USA
No matter results on election day.
Harris or Trump, this game is now over,
Capitalists still roll in green clover.

Loud cheers ring on high from Wall Street windows,
Markets continue to play their bingo.
Forget all those podcast speculations,
Journalists spouting from multi nations,
Whoever is next in through White House door
Stock exchange gamblers will make even more.

Somehow democracy's ceased to matter,
People are angry, beliefs are shattered.
Gaslighters and meme writers down pens,
This rotten charade has come to an end.

4th November 2024

131 - NAUSEOUS OPTIMISM

They're optimistically nauseous.
Has Trump beaten Harris? Of course he has.
Polarisation is new name of game,
Trump's MAGA army share most of blame.

Fag ash fuhrer Farage fawns on Beeb news,
Biden blew it way back, post Covid blues .
Cold winds gather for New Year hand over,
Couch potato proud boys cheer from sofas.

Starmer congratulates, of course he does,
Global sanity rolls under Musk bus.
Tarrifs in back pocket, Bitcoin explodes,
Emporer slips on his tax cutter clothes.

Hawks fly into isolationist walls,
It feels like one more giant kick in balls.

6th November 2024.

132 - AUTHENTIC FELONY

Authentic authoritarians
Fuel their cars with testosterone.
Make America great again,
A slogan that doesn't make sense.

Was America ever great?
Drenched in nuclear riddled blood,
They hold our planet to ransom.
Whither special relationship?

How can we get into his bed?
This felonious cash junky
Moves circus back into White House.
Will Bitcoin supercede dollar?

Billionaire crooks fly higher,
More pavements crack, bridges collapse,
How great is it to see how great
America becomes again?

How quickly slick new motorcades
Of Teslas glide on potholed roads.
Airforce one parties up on high,
Dons dream meme team scribbles more lies,
Legal eagles scrawl alibis,
Who knows who can lead democrats?

Ambassadors get served big macs,
He's got his apron on again,
Whole world seems to have gone insane.

6th November 2024.

133 - ADDICTED TO GROWTH

Facsimile ideas,
Imprinted on our minds,
About democracy,
Filled with historic lies.
There's no opposition
To capitalism.
Fascists bathe in power,
Call neo liberals
Far left as they leave,
Wrapped in abject failure.
War factory chimneys
Belch profits evermore,
Whilst refugees are shown
Exit doors by bigots.
Elon Musk pockets windfall,
Twenty two billion
Dollars in first two days.
"News" media revealed
As continuum hacks,
MAGA emissaries
Revel in new chaos.

As old New Lefts search for
Cracks in global structures
Reality becomes
More visible each hour.
Chained growth addicted dogs
Released unbound to gnaw
On bones of certainty.
All hail fin de siecle
As freedoms ebb away,
Laissez-faire addicts ride
Authoritarian
Rockets backwards into
Power once more today.

Harry Rogers 8th November 2024.

JUXTAPOSITIONS

134 - HOW MUCH LONGER?

We know. Don't we?
Know there is no plan to hand back
Their homes. Don't we?
Northern Gaza will be annexed
Next year. Won't it?
This ongoing theft we stand against,
All planned. Ain't it?

Settlers anticipation grows
With each bomb dropped.
American bombs, German bombs.
Our bombs. Ain't they?
Do we pay taxes to kill kids?
Do we? Do We?
Pay tax to sponsor genocide?
Do we? Do We?

No homes for Palestinians,
That's what we've done.
No food for Palestinians,
Look what we've done.
No schools, no hospitals, no roads,
We watched it all.

Politicians we voted for,
Bankrolled it all,
In Westminster and Washington,
Made it happen.

How much longer can we take this?
How much longer?

8th November 2024

JUXTAPOSITIONS

135 - TELL THE TRUTH

King of fakes, Farage, now apes Trump in Wales.
Reform targets next Sennedd elections.
No doubt his mate Elon will float his boat
As he spreads his banter through valleys.

How can we counter hatred, fear, and lies?
We can't concentrate on lessons unlearnt,
Nor can we chase extreme centrist pipedreams.
Everyone knows we must live in "the now".

No time to rerun failed austerity.
Don't waste resources on mass destruction,
Nor spend our precious time on drone warfare.

With care homes in crisis, NHS too,
Food banks endemic, rent rises too high,
What do we need to do now? TELL THE TRUTH.

10th November 2024.

136 - INPUT-OUTPUT

When will we learn input dictates output?
AI doesn't know what it doesn't know,
A bit like most politicians really.
Search engines, prone to hallucinations,
Rule large areas of our daily lives.

Whilst we invest them fully with our trust,
When we search for answers to hard questions,
More and more hallucinations tick up.
As more fake news sewage is tipped into
Rivers and oceans of human knowledge
Pollution grows and confusion expands.

We are led to believe all things Google,
That they will never, ever, let us down.

Never forget, garbage in garbage out.

10th November 2024

JUXTAPOSITIONS

137 - WHATEVER NEXT?

Is something rotten in America?
How come so many polls got it so wrong?
If what we're told is true hope's under threat,
All of my good friends there are in danger.
Prejudice swaggers along city streets,
Graphically drawn out with every speech.
Elon gibbers and gloats, X marks his spot.
Leaders jockey to gain Trumps bloody ear,
Middle east storm clouds hang heavy and dank,
Israelis threaten to annexe West Bank.
My mirror grows clouded, blocked out by fear,
What kind of greatness will we see or hear?
Nothing is proposed to end genocide,
As ballots came in I sat down and cried.

12th November 2024

JUXTAPOSITIONS

138 - LAISSEZ-FAIRE AUTHORITARIANISM

Laissez-faire authoritarian rule
Seeps into world corridors of power.
Slowly, leaders adopt Thelemic stance,
Where they force us to allow them to act
As Alastair Crowley risen from grave.

Where they become free to do what they wilt
Because their will is the whole of the law.
These parvenu fascist aristocrats,
Drunk on hedonistic bongs of power,
Are determined to destroy rules of law
In order to release themselves from jail.

They pardon each other for former crimes,
Abuse humanity in freedoms name.

These days shape up to be our worst of times.

12th November 2024

139 - GHOST HOUSE KEYS

How many people carry front door keys
To Gazan homes that no longer exist?
Dragooned from area to area,
So many false promises of safety,
Relentlessly on foot, day in, day out,
Carry fewer and fewer possessions,
Many houses gone, obliterated,
Yet still some hope theirs, perhaps, have been spared.

Like their grandparents before them, hold tight
To belief that when this nightmare finishes,
They will once more have family shelter,
With latches that their keys will firmly lock.

These dreams are of ghost houses now bulldozed,
Flattened, scraped away, yet still hope dies last.

16th November 2024.

140 - JUXTAPOSITIONS

Impossible juxtapositions fly
Through my mind and I cannot block them out.
Beauty burns brightly in art galleries.
Colours, shapes, lines, edges softly defined,
Jewellers and potters can all blow my mind,
Exquisitely woven cloths turn me on.
Paintings and drawings made in candlelight,
Bring tears of joy at such re-creation.
Walk on hills through fields down to tree lined streams,
Wildlife continues to inhabit dreams.

All this and yet I'm wracked daily with pain,
Sounds of soldiers as they cheer on their drones,
Such brutalised youth chill all of my bones,
"Another one bites the dust" sung out, loud,
As one more block of homes crashes to ground.
Whole extended families vaporised,
Day in, day out, before our very eyes,
Four year old children, sister and brother,
Hug each other close, they've lost their mother,
Father, uncles, aunts, cousins, grandparents,
All of them obliterated, all gone.
Such bewilderment within their wide eyes,
Now stuck like a gauze filter in my mind.

I know there is still beauty all around,
But guilt haunts my mind, I can't enjoy it,
Nature so defiled I can no longer
Wipe slates clean, erase horrors from my brain.
I see there is still beauty in this world,
But that look in their eyes....... Constantly here.

17th November 2024.

141 - WHAT WE ALL KNOW

Everybody knows what it is called.

That cabbie in Llantrisant,
Shopkeeper in Penrhiwllan,
Postal worker from Llanon,
Those roofers in their white van,
Young barman in Carmarthen,
With his music lover friend,
Red poets in Pontyprydd,
Green activists from Cardiff,
Barrista in Cardigan,
Llanrhystud improvisers,
On guitar, sax, bass, and drums,
Know what politicians hide.

This crime is definitely genocide,
One by one they all told me it is so.

17th November 2024.

142 - THEY'LL DO WHAT THEY WILT IF WE LET THEM

This society is about to become one that protects the will of the few over the rights of the many.

This new political oligarchy that's come into being is almost Thelemic in nature.

What we see are beings like Trump and Musk acting in ways which seem very much akin to "Do what thou wilt shall be the whole of the law", (as written by Alistair Crowley).

However with Trump and Musk this maxim has been transmuted to "We'll do what we wilt shall be the whole of your laws, we'll curtail your rights, and you will obey."

It's time to change that. For the Many, Not the Few still sounds good to me.

Bring on an Eco-Socialist future whilst there's still time.

20th November 2024

JUXTAPOSITIONS

143 - CRYPTO GROWTH TO NOWHERE

Such a giant Ponzi scheme, new in deed.
Fiat control of money disappears,
Along with all our rights and services.

Bitcoin hits one hundred K, world's gone mad.
Musk and his ilk practice their sex magick
On entire planet, we are all fucked now.

Temperatures keep right on going up,
Vultures don't care though, they launch more rockets,
How many die as they fill their pockets?

It's an end in itself that fits neatly,
Watch algorhythms stiff us completely,
Drones watch each move in every city.

Gaza a model of social control.
Ain't no time left now for loud rock and roll.

23rd November, 2024

JUXTAPOSITIONS

144 - SNAPITY SNAP

There's a snap election in Germany,
What happens when right waits ready in wings?
Watch carefully, this ain't one of those things,
Those everyday things, ordinary things.

This is a crisis, politics failure,
Coalition collapses as Trump wins.
Hurricane Donald heads straight for Europe,
Tariffs will cripple across pond exports.
German workers are gaslighted once more.

Put all blame on illegal immigrants,
MAGA populist tropes rolled out anew,
On a global scale fascist hatred spreads,
Main stream media stand and scratch their heads,
Billionaires don't care. Win, win, for them.

25th November 2024

145 - TIME TO WISE UP

Con men with their con tracts
Rain missiles all around,
Gaslight all our people,
Sprinkle destruction down.
Don't care who they blow up,
Don't give a flying fuck,
Long as they make profits,
We've all run out of luck,

Look back to The Sixties,
Celebrity hippies
With flowers in their hair
And rainbows in their eyes
Spread messages of peace
And love in all their songs.
Now there's so much hatred,
Where did we all go wrong?

Those children in Kiev
In Gaza and Sudan,
Wherever there is war
Are ignored by the man.
Guess they always have been
Wherever men spar up,
Where money's to be made
They always fill their cups.

Biden gives his get go,
Then Starmer follows suit,
Zelensky seems joyful,
Arms dealers harvest fruit,
Netanyahu, Putin,
These self proclaimed strong men,
Maintain bomb turnover,
World war three threat again.

In every single year
Since end of World war two
Bombs exploded somewhere
This is what humans do.
Keep each other frightened,

JUXTAPOSITIONS

Too scared to make a fuss,
So long as war ain't here,
And they're not bombing us.

Safeguard our own children,
Focus minds on other,
Spew their propaganda,
Kill another mother.
Nations ununited,
Blow each other to bits,
These legal arms dealers?
Apocalyptic shits.

At deep root of all this
Destruction and despair,
Cosseted shareholders
Put money before care,
On par with drug runners,
Addicted to their trade,
When will we shut them down,
And rain on their parade?

Elbit and QinetiQ
Boeing and Lockheed too
Plus many hundreds more
All exploit me and you.
Take government money,
Those taxes we all paid,
We don't bat an eyelid
Because we're all afraid.

Ain't it time we wised up?

Ain't it time to rise up?

When will we all wise up?

Why won't we all rise up?

25th November 2024

146 - ON OHIO'S STREETS

Fearmongering bigots in Ohio
March bold as brass beneath their swastikas.
Masked up, not brave enough to show faces.

This is third millennium fascism,
Where modern day Nazis strut on our streets,
Emboldened by recent utterances
Of sick Trump/Musk corporate alliance
At mass "Republican" rallies on stump
For destruction of life as we know it.

Project twenty five, drawn from old Berlin,
Designed to open a clear way forward
For ultra rightwing evangelicals
To impose nasty mindset boundaries,
Through American Christian Government.

27th November 2024.

147 - TABLE FOR ONE AT RONNIE'S.

Watch brand new documentary movie,
Ronnie Scott's Soho Jazz Club brought alive,
Rollins, and Davis, Nina and Ella,
Jimi and Georgie, Van the Man and Chet,
They all played there whilst all of us went there.

One time in London, at a conference,
I needed music to empty my head,
Arrive at club to see Madelaine Bell,
"Table for one sir?" they ask at the door.

Say "Sadly yes.", hand over a score,
A waitress is called, she's half of my age,
Leads me in through the crowd, down to the front,
Seats me at table on edge of the stage.

I'm at the table for one at Ronnie's.

17th November 2020.

JUXTAPOSITIONS

148 - 1933 REDUX

Look around at bystanders everywhere.
They watch as freedom drifts slowly skywards,
Libraries filleted of social thought.

Ideas of individuality
Banished from public education spheres.
Endlessly brainwashed by false dreams of rapture,
People are relentlessly gaslighted
From platform after platform by henchmen.

Resurrected dogma dressed up in lies
Spread willy nilly around spot marked X.
President elect turns jokes into fear
Whilst he debases his Thanksgiving speech.

As February quickly approaches
It feels like nineteen thirty three redux.

30th November 2024

JUXTAPOSITIONS

149 - B O M B S

As of January 2024, there were an estimated 12,121 nuclear warheads in the world:
Russia: 5,580 warheads
United States: 5,044 warheads
China: 500 warheads
U K 225 warheads
Other countries: Estimated to have warheads: India, Pakistan, Israel, and North Korea.

B O M B S

Us little mortals are held to ransom
By sick capitalist extortionists
And overblown, self opinionated,
Despotic rulers of horror regimes.

They do this by maintaining subtle fear
Of atomic weapon Armageddon.
Every so often a crank, like Putin,
Threatens to actually detonate
A tactical nuclear missile bomb
On an enemy battlefield somewhere.

We all sit up and pay more attention
To our mainstream media news channels
For a short while, before we resume our
All too important online games routines.

1st December 2024

150 - LOUD RED WARNING

How strong this wind that blocks our roads,
Tears down neighbours leylandii,
Rips roofs from sheds near Llangranog,
Helps turn neat gardens into bogs.

Got loud red warning on my phone,
Did not go out, I stayed at home,
On TV ocean turned to foam,
Hard rain forced down our chimney stack,
Clear up wet mess with bated breath.

We're lucky here, no power cuts,
Thankfully we're not close to death.
I snuggle deeper neath duvet,
How thankful am I here today,
As storm blows on, then blows away.

Meanwhile, in Gaza, genocide
Attrocities go on and on,
Ambulances blown up in siege
On Kamal Aswan hospital,
Israeli strikes kill twenty six
In Nuseirat refugee camp.

Our tempest will blow itself out,
In Palestine death storms rage on.
Red warnings come, red warnings go,
Dead children though, they'll never know.

7th December 2024.

JUXTAPOSITIONS

151 - A CANTERBURY TALE

Archbishop of Canterbury stands up
And cracks jokes for last time in House of Lords.
Behaves as if his demise has nothing
To do with his actions in times gone by.

In his pompous religiosity
View echoes of closed ranks organisations,
Where plush carpet corners are lifted up,
Crimes and misdemeanors swept clean out of view.

How ever he got there to begin with
Is a moot question that nobody ever asks.
Check out his Wikipedia entry,
You'll find he's a full member of Eton
Old Boys club with pretty crazy habits.

Speaks in tongues when he prays, no-one listens!

16th December 2024.

JUXTAPOSITIONS

152 - CHURCH IN LURCH

York joins Canterbury in crass failure,
Expect more grubby glossolalia.
Bucks stop on high evangelical desks
Anglicans defended friends in their mess.

All those young angelic Christian boys
Raped and beaten, paedophiliac toys.
Ugly monsters in loco parentis,
Safeguarded by those in mitres and gowns,
Systematically picked out victims.

Iwerne Trust holiday camps now revealed
As places unsafe for public school kids.
False Bishop tears stolen from crocodiles.
Yet still elites blare out their songs of praise,
From cathedrals where they don't change their ways.

17th December 2024

JUXTAPOSITIONS

153 - DEREK ROARS ON

Derek flies along High Street from Three Comps,
Swings around Belisha beacon at speed,
Spurts across zebra, manic grin on face,
Obviously a man on a mission.

As he speeds past I lower car window,
Shout out "Hello Derek", he does not hear.
I drive on, park up, and we go shopping.

Just before we reach Emlyn Post Office
Derek charges towards us grin intact,
As his fingers deftly manipulate

Levers on arm of electric wheelchair
He weaves his legless body through hard rain.

He sees me, grin broadens, I say "Hello",
"Can't stop, it's pissing down." Derek roars on.

18th December 2024

154 - KIMONO DRAGONS

Something happens when I write a poem,
My thoughts, collective, put in perspective.
Try hard to focus in on each topic,
Feeling, thought, picture, vision, as I type.

Each time I start a brand new piece of work,
I know not how my words appear early,
Amazement grows as work fills up my page,
Here find beauty, solace in my old age.

My mirror reflects imagination
Stirred into vortex of reality.

I allow my mind to wander at will,
Realise whole world has become surreal,
More and more write exactly what I feel,
Dragons in kimonos sugar my pill.

19th December 2024

155 - CROSS THAT LINE

What happens when you cross that line
Cross that line
Cross that line
When new friendship turns into love
Cross that line
Cross that line
You never know when love will hit
Cross that line
Cross that line
Nothing you can do to stop it
Cross that line
Cross that line
One night when we were in that bar
Cross that line
Cross that line
You looked at me a certain way
Cross that line
Cross that line
I could not turn my gaze away
Cross that line
Cross that line
Nothing ever be same again
Cross that line
Cross that line
Electric touches of our hands
Cross that line
Cross that line
Forty two years across that line
Cross that line
Cross that line
Still together across that line
Cross that line
Cross that line
Our love still strong across that line
Cross that line
Cross that line

19th December 2024

JUXTAPOSITIONS

156 - DIALECTICAL HOLIDAY

Storms rage on in cities flattened by war,
Wolves howl in deepest mental recesses,
Wreckage of what were once communities
Lies strewn willy nilly where once we danced.

In Syria American bombs fall,
Launched by Israel as bloodbaths deepen.
Here bells jingle, trees sparkle, tunes jangle,
Coloured chains sway across party ceilings,
Our children showered with love filled feelings,
All around tables groan with winter feasts,
Palestinians starve in Middle East.

In Florida egos seem fit to burst,
My heart aches, there's too much pain, my brain hurts.

Just one more dialectical Christmas.

Harry Rogers 20th December 2024.

JUXTAPOSITIONS

157 - RUN HELL FOR LEATHER

With a death stick in his lips
He shows he's a lunatic
Uses Musk's algorithmic tricks
To take Sennedd in twenty six.

We head towards heavy weather
If we don't get our act together.
Almost at end of my tether,
We gotta run hell for leather

Run, run, run, run, run
Run hell for leather
We gotta
Run, run, run, run, run
Run hell for leather

They'll use fear and paranoia,
Trumped up lies to scare us all,
Meanwhile uptown in Whitehall
Starmer and his pals do fuck all.

When all our hedgerows overgrow,
More Nazis preach on radio,
Time runs out before we know,
There's nowhere left for us to go.

All we can do is stand up tall
Let them know that we won't fall
Our candidates are not so small
We're gonna run and beat them all.

Run, run, run, run, run
Run hell for leather
We gonna
Run, run, run, run, run
Run hell for leather

We're gonna run and beat them all.
Farage? He's heading for a fall.

JUXTAPOSITIONS

Run, run, run, run, run
Run hell for leather
We gonna
Run, run, run, run, run
Run hell for leather
Let's stand together!

21st December 2024.

JUXTAPOSITIONS

158 - BEST OF DAYS

Into darkness beneath thickest night clouds
Where arms of Morpheus are strapped to sides,
Noise of unmanned aerial vehicles rules,
Vibrations tremble thinnest canvas walls.

Explosions echo nonstop near and far.
Dreams undreamt, forever lost, drift away.
Here within our thin veneer we await
With great tremulous anticipation
Our annual best of days where families
Remember who we are and why we love.

Over indulge in favourite pleasures,
Share out gifts of valued future treasures.
Our memories of all these best of days
Hide collective action realities.

Baby Jesus dead in Gazan rubble,
All infrastructure blown to fucking bits,
Remember this as you take pampered shits,
On these, our very, very, best of days.

23rd December 2024

JUXTAPOSITIONS

159 - MUSKRAT HATE

MUSKRAT HATE (Redux)

Muskrat, Muskrat broad daylight
Gamin' the town and gamin' it right
In the evenin', not very pleasin'

Muskrat crazy, Muskrat mad
Does his jitterbug
With Trump in Muskrat land
Watch them shimmy
Through their hominy

And they lie and they spin and smash quangos
Whingin' and fiddlin' old plan Joe
Floatin' above Mexico's gate
Looks like Muskrat hate

Nibblin' our bacon, chewin' our cheese
Don says to Elon
Hey Man, would you please bankroll my game?
Elon he says yes, he has no shame

Now, he's ticklin' Don's fancy
Wearin' his ties
Muzzle to muzzle now
Anything goes
As they wiggle
Don starts to giggle

And they lie and they spin where they can go
Whingin' and fiddlin' old plan Joe
Floatin' up above Greenland's gate
Looks like Muskrat hate

And they lie and they spin where they can go
Whingin' and fiddlin' old plan Joe
Floatin' above Panama's gate
Looks like Muskrat hate

Don, Don, Don, Don, don't
Don't, do-e, don't

JUXTAPOSITIONS

Elon, Elon, don't
Don't, do-e, don't
Don't, don't, don't, don't, don't
Don't, do-e, don't
Don't, don't, don't, don't, don't

27th December 2024

JUXTAPOSITIONS

160 - SQUARE PEGS, ROUND HOLES

In school days I was a
Square peg in a round hole
I never got it on
Never did my homework
I just didn't belong
Even now seldom fit
Always go my own way
Find it hard to obey.

To those many
Square pegs
Stuck inside
Round holes
Do not worry
You're fine
Please don't worry
It's fine

Always ask this question
Whenever things get tough
Do they ever listen?
If your answer is no
You know enough's enough.
When teachers ignore you
And your parents do too
Find someone else who will.

Jump up all you
Square pegs
Leap out of those
Round holes
Tell your story
Shout loud
Make them listen
Shout loud

Square pegs stuck in round holes
Tell what is happening
Square pegs stuck in round holes
It's time to change your world
Square pegs stuck in round holes

JUXTAPOSITIONS

Don't let them hammer you
Square pegs stuck in round holes
Show everyone it's you

Jump up all you
Square pegs
Leap out of those
Round holes
Tell your story
Shout loud
Make them listen
Shout loud

29th December 2024

JUXTAPOSITIONS

161 - FORWARD HE WALKS

In wreckage of last Gazan hospital
A brave doctor emerges from rubble.
Forward he walks towards IDF tanks,
His white coat pristine against smashed concrete.

Still our media refuse to nail flags
To their mastheads and call out genocide.
Dead patients stretchered out for burial,
Survivors, bewildered by finality,
Shepherded into heighth of wretchedness.

North Gaza, where water has been cut off,
Sewage removal infrastructure gone,
Housing reduced By eighty three percent,
Majority of roads unuseable,
Food sporadically available.

Our politics in New Normal are fucked,
Bombed hospitals are deemed un-newsworthy.
I have never felt so angry as this.
Humans? Something is gone awry I fear.
Evolution or Armageddon, eh?

Meanwhile an old man dies aged one hundred
And every editor goes crazy.........

Harry　　　　　Rogers　　　　　30th　　　　　December　　　　　2024.

Printed in Great Britain
by Amazon